WILLIE'S WAY

PHILLIP VAN HOOSER

WILLIE'S WAY

6 Secrets for Wooing, Wowing, and
WINNING CUSTOMERS AND THEIR LOYALTY

© Copyright 2019 – The Revocable Trust for Phillip Van Hooser

All rights reserved. This book is protected by the copyright laws of the United States of America. No part of this publication may be reproduced, stored in or introduced into a retrieval system, or transmitted, in any form or by any means (electronic, mechanical, photocopying, recording or otherwise), without the prior written permission of the publisher. For permissions requests, contact the publisher, addressed "Attention: Permissions Coordinator," at the address below.

Published and Distributed by
SOUND WISDOM
PO Box 310
Shippensburg, PA 17257-0310
717-530-2122

info@soundwisdom.com

www.soundwisdom.com

While efforts have been made to verify information contained in this publication, neither the author nor the publisher assumes any responsibility for errors, inaccuracies, or omissions. While this publication is chock-full of useful, practical information, it is not intended to be legal or accounting advice. All readers are advised to seek competent lawyers and accountants to follow laws and regulations that may apply to specific situations. The reader of this publication assumes responsibility for the use of the information. The author and publisher assume no responsibility or liability whatsoever on the behalf of the reader of this publication.

The scanning, uploading and distribution of this publication via the Internet or via any other means without the permission of the publisher is illegal and punishable by law. Please purchase only authorized editions and do not participate in or encourage piracy of copyrightable materials.

Library of Congress Control Number:

2012936032

Previously published under ISBN: 978-1-893322-83-7

ISBN 13 TP: 978-1-64095-144-0

ISBN 13 eBook: 978-1-64095-145-7

For Worldwide Distribution, Printed in the U.S.A.

3 4 5 6 / 21 20

Praise for... *Willie's Way*

"*Willie's Way* is pure GOLD...entertaining, educational and loaded with words of wisdom, presented with insight and sparkling good humor. It's food for thought, nourishment for the spirit and contains stuff that will stick to your ribs."

Bob Mann, President
Club Marketing Services, Inc.

"Along comes *Willie's Way* and I'm reminded once again that when it comes to making customers happy, it's still the basics that really matter. Every page contains a nugget to be picked up, examined, appreciated and put in a visible place where it can serve as a daily reminder that Willie knows how to drive true success."

Marilynn T. Mobley, Senior Vice President
and Strategic Counsel, Edelman

"Phillip Van Hooser delivers a passionate message on customer service...a passionate message with real life stories, proving that inspiration comes from unexpected people in the least expected places."

Steve Powless, President, CEO
Computer Services, Inc. (CSI)

"Phillip Van Hooser has captured the essence of customer service through his exhilarating delivery of personal anecdotes coupled with timeless fundamentals. I recommend this book for anyone who has an interest in improving their own or their organization's level of customer service."

Greg Burden, Senior Account Executive
Training & Capability Enhancement
Proctor & Gamble Pharmaceuticals

"*Willie's Way* is an invaluable tool that is a must for everyone in the service industry."

Shelly Foxworthy, First Vice President
Medicare Audit & Reimbursement,
Mutual of Omaha

"Phillip Van Hooser is the ultimate 'service champion.' With *Willie's Way* he shows how top service wins in an increasingly competitive world."

Tom Moser, Vice Chairman, KPMG LLP

"Phillip Van Hooser's perspective on attracting customers is a pragmatic way to emphasize the key factors of success with any customer. He has proven that customer relations is simple, while we work to make it complicated. I would recommend *Willie's Way* to anyone who has customer relations as a part of their life or who appreciates good stories. Not only can this book teach you the power of customer focus, Phillip Van Hooser's storytelling talent is filled with clever insights that can't help but educate and entertain."

Jerry Armstrong, President
CVG Americas

"This book is a must read for all! *Willie's Way* shows you how to bring out your fullest potential so you can make a positive difference in this life by creating special memories in every life you touch. Success in life can be yours if you will follow 'Willie's way!'"

Mia Kosasa, Vice President
Bradley Pacific Aviation

"Phillip Van Hooser encourages and suggests to his readers to brand and personalize service—avoiding the cookie cutter approach. He challenges us to be innovative and creative, thereby creating a winning situation for the customer and the organization."

Bonnie A. McElearney, Director
Employee Development, Atmos Energy

"Just as he connected with Willie Watson, Phillip Van Hooser has a unique gift in his ability to connect with people at all levels in any organization. He takes leadership and customer service principles which can be difficult to practice on a daily basis and communicates them clearly and in a common sense manner so that everyone can relate them to their own situation."

Dan Daniel, Group Executive
Danaher Motion

"Unleashing the principles of *Willie's Way* on a group of employees like ours with a common focus has value that will grow with each customer encounter."

Stephen K. Wiggins, Chief Information Officer
BlueCross BlueShield South Carolina

*Susan, thank you for believing in me.
I am anxious to see what our next
twenty years together will bring.*

Table of Contents

Acknowledgments ix

Introduction: Make the Ordinary Extraordinary 1

Secret #1: Acknowledge Your Customers Immediately 19
    What Is a Customer? 21
    Opportunities Lost 23
    The Game of Service Is the Game of Business 29
    He'll Know My Name 31
    Putting It Into Practice 33

Secret #2: Redefine Your Routine Activities 37
    A Finishing School for Motorcycle Cops 39
    A Service Pro at Work in Terminal A 46
    The 999 Drill 49
    Putting It Into Practice 50

Secret #3: Give Customers Your Undivided Attention 53
    Hey! Welcome to Cici's! 55
    We Escort Our Guests 57
    A Sign of the Times 60
    It's Simple—Service Sells 63
    Putting It Into Practice 66

Secret #4: Listen, Think, and Use Common Sense 69
    I Prefer Peach Yogurt 71
    Service Is Spelled S-A-Z-E-R-A-C 74
    When Is a Greeter Not Just a Greeter? 77
    Service Is Common Sense 80
    Putting It Into Practice 84

Table of Contents

Secret #5: Bend the Rules, Sometimes 87
    Take a Minute to Think 91
    He Will If He Really Wants to Sell Me Something 95
    I Guess This Is My Lucky Day 98
    Putting It in Practice 103

Secret #6: Make the Last Few Seconds Count 105
    You Don't Expect Us to Give Our Services Away, Do You? 106
    They Try Harder and It Pays 110
    Well, I'll Be Doggone 114
    Making Friends by Serving Friends 117
    Putting It in Practice 119

Conclusion: The Magic of Service Professionalism 121
    When Magic Isn't Magic After All 124
    Magic Defined 127
    Mythical Customer Service 128
    It Can't Get "Mulch" Worse Than That 131
    Experiencing a Magical Moment 135

About the Author 139

Service Professionalism in Action 141

Acknowledgments

Willie Watson's personal example of selfless service not only inspired me to write this book, it continues to inspire me to be a better customer servant. I sincerely appreciate Willie's enthusiasm for this project and his encouragement to have me share our experience with others.

Susan has been my wife, business partner, and most honest supporter for over 20 years. She has heard more of my service stories—good and bad—than most could even imagine or tolerate. My work is built on the foundation of her love and continuing support.

Thank you to Whitney Campbell for her design expertise and guidance. What a pleasure you have been to work with. I'm looking forward to the next project together.

Finally, to the hundreds of service professionals who have attended to my needs as a consumer over the years—thank you. A smaller number, many of whom are mentioned in the following pages, have made an indelible impression on me and my personal commitment to service professionalism. To each, whether named or forever anonymous, I continue to be grateful.

Willie's Way

Introduction

Make the Ordinary Extraordinary

*Hey, buddy. Need a ride?
I've been sittin' here waitin' for ya.*
— Willie Watson

I wasn't expecting much really. In fact, after 20 years and more than two million miles of business travel, if anything, I had come to expect the worst. Delayed flights, lost baggage, overbooked hotels, undercooked meals, detached, sometimes surly service providers. I had experienced them all. It seemed like at every turn, I came face-to-face with disappointing and dispassionate service. There was simply no reason to expect today would be any different. But it was.

As wants and needs go, mine were simple. As I sat in that aisle seat of the coach section of a crowded 737, I allowed myself a few minutes to daydream. *As tough as this day has been, I'll still be happy if I can get a quick, pleasant ride from the airport to the hotel, a good hot meal, and a relaxing night's rest.*

A fairly basic expectation? Yes. A sure thing? Hardly.

It had been a grueling day already. My hotel wakeup call had come at 3:45 a.m. Less than 45 minutes later I was standing, bleary-eyed, in the hotel lobby waiting for the shuttle that would take me to the San Francisco International Airport for my 6:00 a.m. flight.

I scheduled the shuttle pickup at the same time that I requested my wakeup call the night before. The desk clerk made it perfectly clear that the

1

hotel's shuttles only made airport runs on the half-hour. "Absolutely, no exceptions," she stressed. Therefore, if I missed the 4:30 a.m. shuttle I would have to wait until 5:00 a.m. for the next shuttle cycle, she warned. In my mind, five o'clock would be cutting it much too close to allow adequate time to get checked in for a six o'clock flight. Therefore, my options were limited. Either be there by 4:30 a.m.—or take a cab. I opted for the lesser of two evils. I was standing in the lobby at 4:25. The shuttle finally arrived at 4:40.

I made my 6:00 a.m. flight. This cross-country jaunt from San Francisco to Atlanta left on time and arrived on time. However, after the requisite 60-minute layover in Atlanta, my second flight's scheduled departure time to Columbia, South Carolina, had been pushed back once, then twice, and finally a third time before we were allowed to board. The reason for the delay was never clear, because it was never communicated. Despite the inconvenience to the passengers, we were simply told to wait (patiently) in the gate area for further notice, because the "status of the flight was uncertain and could change at any time." Finally, an hour and a half past the scheduled departure time, we found ourselves airborne, winging our way to South Carolina's capital city and my final destination for the day.

Though I had only been up and traveling for about 10 hours, it felt like it had been days. The bone-numbing flights, coupled with the incessant waiting had begun to take their toll on me. It was a Saturday, after a long week of traveling. I was tired. I was frustrated. And there wasn't a thing in the world I could do about any of it. I was at the mercy of others.

In search of a reprieve from my current reality, I allowed myself the luxury of closing my eyes and briefly losing myself in a fanciful daydream about a fairytale travel land far, far away. A land where the customer mattered and was never taken for granted. A land where companies promised less and delivered more, instead of promising much more and delivering considerably less. A land where uncomplicated cab rides, hot meals, and relaxing hotel stays were the bare bones minimum in professional service instead of an almost unrealistic expectation.

Make The Ordinary Extraordinary

As the airplane's wheels returned to earth, my thoughts returned to the reality around me. Soon I was standing in the baggage claim area located in the bowels of the Columbia airport. Though my bags normally were reunited with me upon arrival at my various travel destinations, I had learned over the years not to take that simple expected outcome for granted. I was able to recall too many occasions when, for various reasons, my bags had arrived hours and even days after me. Giving a speech to a corporate audience while dressed in jeans and tennis shoes or rushing to a local mall in a desperate, last minute search for presentable business attire were not my idea of fun activities.

So there I stood, watching anxiously as bags of every size and shape came spilling off the conveyor belt and onto the revolving metal carousel. The seconds clicked away as I stood staring at the strange assortment of bags passing before me. With each new bag, I felt myself becoming more and more ill at ease.

Maybe my bags didn't make it on this flight after all. Maybe there wasn't enough room. Maybe there was a weight issue and my bags are still sitting on the tarmac in Atlanta. Maybe . . .

These unsettling thoughts were arrested with the first sighting of one of my two checked bags. I began to relax a bit as I watched it tumbling toward me. *If one made it, surely the other did, too. Seconds later my other bag emerged from the depths of the baggage handling chasm. My bags made it—maybe this day is going to turn out to be pretty good after all.*

Upon retrieving my luggage and with newfound optimism, I made my way to the courtesy board located adjacent to the baggage carousel. The board was crowded with advertisements and listings for various hotels, motels, rental car agencies, and shuttle services. As I scoured the display, my eyes finally found what I was looking for—the hotel where my reservation had been made. Beneath the picture of my soon-to-be home-away-from-home were the words: TO SCHEDULE FREE SHUTTLE SERVICE, USE THE COURTESY PHONE AND DIAL 13. I cradled the phone receiver in my left hand as my

Willie's Way

right index finger punched the "1," then the "3" button as instructed. After the second ring, a female voice with a distinctive Southern accent answered.

"Thank you for calling the [name withheld to protect the guilty] Hotel. This is Trisha. How may I direct your call?"

"Hello, Trisha. My name is Phillip Van Hooser. I have a reservation at your hotel for this evening and I will be checking in shortly. I'm at the airport now. Would you please send your shuttle out here to pick me up?"

"I'm sorry, sir. We don't offer shuttle service from the airport."

"Excuse me?" I said somewhat confused. "I don't understand. I'm standing at the courtesy board at the airport right now. I'm looking at your listing as we speak. It says for free shuttle service I should dial 13. I dialed 13 and now I'm talking to you," I said, as I noticed the volume of my voice rise a few decibels and the tone an octave or two.

On the other end of the line, the young woman gave no indication that she recognized or appreciated my confusion or growing level of frustration. Rather it seemed to be just another day at the office for her. Her response was offered in a matter-of-fact manner.

"Sir, we don't offer shuttle service from the airport," she said again, as if repeating the message would make it somehow more palatable the second time around. Then she added almost cheerfully, "I don't know why they don't take that advertisement off that board. Anyway, I guess you'll just have to catch a cab. See you soon. Bye-bye."

The line went dead.

I hung up the phone with more than a trace of disgust. *Welcome to Columbia. We love travelers. We're glad you're here, I thought. Another pitiful example of service expectations not met.*

My options now severely limited, I grudgingly shouldered my luggage and began to make my way toward the airport exit and the crush of cabs that I knew would be waiting outside.

Make The Ordinary Extraordinary

I've ridden in hundreds of cabs over the years, but I've never learned to enjoy the experience. I've always viewed a cab ride as an occasional, unavoidable necessity. Granted, cabs are usually quicker and less expensive than renting a car. I admit it's easier to let someone else do the driving in unfamiliar surroundings. And cabs are somewhat more comfortable than being packed like sardines into a multiple-destination, multiple-stop shuttle van. Still, there is much I don't like about the taxi cab experience.

As a general rule, I don't like traveling to unfamiliar cities, climbing into unfamiliar vehicles, being taken to unfamiliar destinations, by unfamiliar drivers—while I pay handsomely for the privilege! On top of all that, more often than not, and contrary to the basic premise of the free enterprise system, at airports I don't even get the option of selecting the driver with whom I choose to do business. For efficiency sake, airport traffic stewards have embraced the FIFO method of taxicab management—First In, First Out. In other words, the next passenger who arrives gets the next available cab. It's as simple as that. No questions asked. As a customer, if you don't like the system, please step out of line and find another mode of transportation, because that's the way it works around here, buddy. For passengers, "FIFO" might more appropriately be spelled "POT LUCK."

Over the years, I have had the personal misfortune of riding in cabs whose drivers were dirty, rude, uncommunicative, obnoxious, profane, threatening, solicitous, unintelligible, sullen, lazy, angry, intimidating—pick your favorite. On several occasions, you would be correct in picking more than one of these characteristics to describe the same driver.

In New Orleans, my cab driver's breath reeked of the unmistakable odor of alcohol. In Chicago, while stopped and waiting on an on-ramp for traffic to clear before merging onto a major freeway, my driver fell fast asleep at the wheel— engine still running, foot (temporarily at least) on the brake. I had to wake him for us to continue. In Dallas, I boarded a cab at the airport, rode all the way into the city, disembarked, and paid my fare—all without the driver ever uttering a single word. Not even a single syllable! A New York City cab driver I was riding with was involved in a minor fender bender. Without ever coming to a complete stop or exiting his vehicle to speak with the driver he had rear-ended, he simply rolled down his window, hurled a profanity-laced tirade at the offended driver and sped away.

I realize these are extreme situations and not the norm as they relate to cab drivers as a whole. However, over the years, I have had so many unpleasant experiences compared to so few pleasant ones, that I have come to expect the worst from the experience even when it (thankfully) does not materialize.

With such dour thoughts in mind, I exited the terminal in anticipation of the inevitable. It's safe to assume I was not a happy traveler.

As I stepped forth into the sunlight, the first thing I noticed was the lack of waiting cabs. *Since I was late getting my bags, maybe the mad rush is over.* In fact, I noticed only one idle cab waiting at the curb, its driver leaned against the car's front quarter panel, his arms crossed, his head bowed low, and his chin tucked securely into his chest. He looked to me as if he might be sleeping. I slowly began to make my way toward him, while still wrestling with my luggage.

As I drew closer to my waiting chariot, I began the process of sizing up my driver. First impressions being what they are, I was fairly confident that he had never read *Dress for Success*. His clothes were simple, clean, but worn. The driver's most notable fashion accessory was a well-worn, brushed leather hat, with the bill pulled down low over his brow. It struck me as an interesting cross between an aviator's hat and the old-style motorcyclist's caps made popular by the likes of Marlon Brando in *The Wild Bunch* decades ago.

Just beneath the bill of his hat, I noticed weathered features, the likes of which come with age, hard work, and multiple life experiences. I had seen faces like this before on the farmers and carpenters, small town politicians and merchants that I grew up around. As my eyes traveled farther down his face, I noticed his almost walrus-like mustache. It was long and bushy, predominantly white as a result of his advancing years, but with a noticeably light red streak. Like a racing stripe, it extended vertically just under his nose. The mustache reached well over his upper lip, its fullness partially hiding his mouth. I guessed him to be in his mid- to late-sixties. He would have been the type of man that would have been easy to look past on a crowded sidewalk. But I couldn't look past him. He represented my immediate means of local transportation.

As I drew closer, he noticed me. He spoke first.

"Hey, buddy. Need a ride?"

His manner was casual and his voice friendly. Still I wasn't in the best of moods. *I should be boarding a free shuttle to the hotel right now.*

"Yeah, I guess I do."

"Good. I've been sittin' here waitin' for ya," he said with a smile in his voice, as he made his way toward me, reaching for my luggage. "I'll load these in the trunk. You can go ahead and make yourself comfortable in the car."

Waiting for me? Yeah, right. Make myself comfortable? He's not concerned about my comfort. He's like all the rest. All he cares about is his fare. Who does this guy take me for? He's desperate. He's trying too hard. No cab driver is really this friendly. He's got some kind of an angle. He's up to something. I'd better watch this guy.

As I relinquished my bags, I asked rather defensively, "Do you have a problem with me sitting up front with you?"

Though I can't explain why, I've always preferred to be in the front seat where the action is. Yet, many cab drivers don't like it. Some will say it's against company policy, especially in big city areas where violent crimes against cab drivers are not uncommon. I've found most drivers just view it as an aggravation—an invasion of their personal space. If a passenger joins them up front, they will have to move their stuff around. Heaven forbid! I was anxious to hear how this driver would handle my request. His response was straightforward and uncomplicated.

"Not at all. Suit yourself. Sit wherever you'll be most comfortable," he said, without a hint of resignation.

Hummh. That was much too easy.

As he finished loading my bags, I took my place in the front seat, opposite the driver and assumed the "shotgun" position. I was in place when I heard the trunk slam shut. Seconds later the driver climbed in and assumed his position behind the wheel. Out of the corner of my eye, I watched as he reached forward for the ignition switch and started the engine. But, before putting the car in gear, he did something totally unexpected. He shifted in his seat and turned his body to face me, while extending his open hand toward me. It was the first time I had looked into his eyes.

"My name is William Watson. My friends call me Willie. I'd appreciate it if you'd call me Willie, too," he said cheerfully.

I didn't mean to be rude. Really I didn't. But this cab driver's display of gregariousness and informality caught me temporarily off guard. Never before had I seen a cab driver take the initiative to introduce himself or herself to me. It happened so quickly and unexpectedly that it took a few seconds for me to process exactly what was happening. All the while, Willie sat patiently, even serenely, behaving as if he had seen this reaction before. His eyes remained fixed on mine, a smile partially buried beneath his mustache, his hand extended.

Soon enough, my manners returned. I reached out, took Willie's hand in mine and shook it. "Hello, Willie. My name is Phillip Van Hooser. My friends call me Phil. It would be nice if you called me Phil, too."

"It's nice to meet ya, Phil."

With the introductions concluded, Willie released my hand and in the same motion reached for the knob on his two-way radio, the same radio that

Make The Ordinary Extraordinary

connected him to his base dispatcher. With a quick flick of the wrist, he turned the radio off.

"That thing is for gettin' customers. It's not for worryin' 'em once I get 'em. You don't mind do ya, Phil?"

I just smiled weakly and said, "No, I don't mind at all."

"Good. Phil, where ya headed?"

"To the [name still withheld] Hotel."

"I know it well. Just sit back and relax and I'll have ya there in about 25 or 30 minutes," Willie said, as he put the cab in gear and pulled away from the curb.

Though we had only been together for a couple of minutes, it was already obvious to me that there was something markedly different about this man as compared to every other cab driver I had ever encountered. There was something special about him and his approach to his business. But what was it? I was curious. I wanted to know more. I needed to keep him talking.

"Willie, have you been busy today?" I asked casually.

Now, this was a perfect example of what I call a "throw away" or "filler" question. The answer to such a question—regardless of what it is—really doesn't matter much to me. We all have several such questions ready to be used at a moment's notice. Though to some they may seem shallow and self-serving, they serve a distinctive purpose in casual conversation. They fill uncomfortable gaps or allow the other person unspoken permission to keep talking.

We all ask throwaway questions periodically like, "How are you doing?" "What's new?" or "Beautiful day, isn't it?" If honesty prevailed, in most cases, we would have to admit that we have very little interest in how the person is *really doing, what's new in their life, or how beautiful* their day might be. Instead, such questions are used to be polite, or in my case, just to keep Willie talking.

Willie's Way

Willie didn't seem to care what my motive was for asking the question. With a simple gesture, he pointed over his shoulder to the cabs that were moving forward into their newly staged positions, aligning themselves for their turn at future incoming travelers.

"No, I haven't been busy at all. In fact, you're my first customer today, Phil. I've been sittin' in that line waitin' for ya since noon."

I quickly stole a glance at my watch and saw that it was now 4:40 p.m. By his own admission, Willie had spent more than four and a half hours waiting for his first fare of the day! Yet, no griping about how bad a day it had been. No complaints about his choice of professions. Not even a hint of noticeable frustration in his voice regarding his lot in life. Willie seemed totally content to focus on the present, not the circumstances associated with his immediate past.

As we drove, Willie began to ask questions. His questions, however, didn't seem to be of the throw away variety at all. He asked each sincerely and listened intently to the answers I offered. They came in rapid succession.

"Phil, is this your first time to Columbia?" "Where do ya live?" "Do ya have a family?" "How much time do ya spend traveling?" and so on.

For several miles we just rode, engaged in what may have seemed to some to be inconsequential chit-chat. Then Willie asked the question I suspect he had been working toward all along.

"Phil, what brings ya to Columbia, anyhow?"

"I'm here on business."

"If ya don't mind my askin', what kind of business are ya in?"

"I'm a professional speaker. I help organizations with leadership and service issues. I'm in town to speak to a group tomorrow morning."

"Ya know, I carry speakers to and from the airport every now and then. Who ya talkin' to tomorrow?"

Make The Ordinary Extraordinary

I began to explain that the organization was a submarine sandwich franchise operation with restaurants located throughout the southeast. However, since I lived outside their service area, I had never visited any of their stores.

"Oh, I know the company well," Willie assured me. "They seem to be a fine bunch. When ya do get the chance to eat there, I suggest ya try a #4—it's my favorite."

I chuckled quietly to myself. *Who is this storehouse of information that's ferrying me to my hotel, anyway?*

"Phil, what are ya gonna be talkin' about tomorrow?"

"I'll be talking to a group of franchise owners and restaurant managers about how to improve customer service in their stores." Then I added, "What about it, Willie? Is there anything you think I need to tell them?"

"Oh, Phil, I wouldn't have any idea about that kinda thing," Willie replied sincerely. "They hired ya. You must be the expert. I'm sure ya got lots of good stuff to tell 'em that'll help 'em out."

We drove on for several more miles engaged in casual conversation. Finally, after more than 20 minutes in the car with Willie, he announced that we were less than five minutes from my destination. Then he began the series of questions that soon led me to realize the full magnitude of his special brand of customer service.

"Phil, when ya leavin' town?"

"Tomorrow, as soon as my program is over," I replied. "I'm scheduled to finish at noon and I need to be at the airport by 1:30 p.m."

"Will ya be headed home?" he asked.

"No, Willie, I'm flying to Phoenix. I'm speaking to another group there first thing Monday morning."

"Well, how do ya plan to get back to the airport?"

11

Willie's Way

I smiled to myself at the obvious implication of this question. Willie was sharp. He was a businessman. He was an entrepreneur. And I was proud of him.

How many times over the years had I reminded groups of sales professionals that two critical keys to effective salesmanship have always been and will always be establishing a personal relationship and then asking for the sale? It's a fact. People enjoy doing business with people they know and like. The personal connection seems to help remove some of the uncertainty from the business relationship. Still, human beings as a whole are cautious by nature—hesitant to take the initiative, hesitant to act. I have found that often, all it takes to get a necessary deal done is to be bold enough to ask for the sale. I shudder to think how many times a deal is left undone and money left on the table simply because no one was bold enough to ask for it. It was obvious to me that Willie understood this principle.

Willie had been systematically getting to know me for the past 20 minutes. He had been asking good questions and listening carefully to my answers. He had a service he believed I needed. Now the time was drawing near for him to close the sale. I was anxious to hear his approach.

"Well, Willie, to answer your question, I guess I'll have to take a cab."

"Phil, let's talk about that for a minute. First thing ya need to know is that gettin' a cab on a Sunday 'round here could be a challenge. We're sittin' here, smack dab in the heart of the Bible belt. Heck, Columbia, South Carolina, may be the *buckle* of the Bible belt. Anyway, not all cab drivers around here work on Sundays. And many of the ones who do, have regular customers they carry to and from church and then to and from dinner after church. Now, Phil, I'm not sayin' that ya won't be able to get a cab tomorrow after your program. I'm just sayin' it won't be nearly as easy as it was today."

Willie sat quietly for a few more seconds, as if deep in thought. He knew my needs as well as I did. He was content to let the silence do its work. The full magnitude of his words and the message they conveyed began to settle into my consciousness. Finally, he cut his eyes over at me and continued.

Make The Ordinary Extraordinary

"Phil, I'll tell ya what I'm willin' to do. If ya want me to, I'll be sittin' out in front of your hotel tomorrow at 12 noon sharp waitin' on ya. Then I'll get ya back to the airport safe and on time so ya can go on to Arizona and make a livin' to support your family. How's that sound to ya?"

"Willie, it sounds fine, except for one thing. I'm not sure what time I'll actually be able to leave. Like I said, my program is scheduled to be over at noon, but sometimes people want to stand around and talk to me after I finish."

Willie interrupted me before I could resist further.

"Stop right there, Phil. If that's all you're worried about, I can help ya out. I'll be at the hotel at noon. If ya don't come out 'til 12:30, no problem. If ya don't come out 'til 1:00, I'll still be waitin'. Heck, Phil, if ya don't come out 'til 3:00 o'clock, I'll STILL be sittin' in this cab waitin' on ya."

"Now ya need to know something—I don't do this for everybody. Ya probably never would've thought about it, but not everybody likes cab drivers. In fact, some people wouldn't think twice about standin' a driver up—just leave 'em sittin' there by the curb, with no idea that the customer has already gone."

Then Willie turned to face me once more. "But, I don't believe you'd do that to me, would ya, Phil?"

I felt my face flush. *So there are other folks like me out there who aren't big fans of cab drivers. Apparently, they haven't met this guy yet.*

"Uhm, no Willie, uh, I wouldn't do that to you," I stammered, somewhat sheepishly.

"Good. Then what do ya think? Ya want me to come get ya or not?"

"Willie, I think it's an outstanding idea. Just one less thing I'll have to worry about. I'll be looking forward to seeing you tomorrow, sometime after noon."

About that time, we pulled into the hotel parking lot and up to the front door. We got out of the cab and Willie fetched my bags from the trunk. I paid him his fare, plus a generous tip. *If ever a cab driver deserved a generous tip, this one did,* I thought.

Then I watched as he climbed back into his mobile office. I watched as he turned his two-way radio back on, reconnecting himself with his marketplace. And I watched as he drove away in search of his next customer service opportunity.

With Willie gone, I stepped into the lobby of my lodging place for the night. I approached the registration counter hoping for a better service experience than my earlier telephone call had provided. Unfortunately, I was disappointed again. The poor service attitude and lack of focus regarding this customer's (and I assume others') needs was laughable at best and downright frustrating at worst. I could share two other specific examples of service opportunities gone very wrong that I experienced while in this hotel. But to do so, might be interpreted as a blatant case of "piling on." Suffice it to say that despite the name recognition, fancy trappings, and expansive staff, this was an organization suffering from SAD—service attention deficiency—and *sad* it was!

Of course, the hotel's service problems were magnified in my mind as I unavoidably compared the lack of service I was receiving at the hotel to the special brand of service I had received from Willie. On the one hand, the hotel had promised more and delivered less. Willie, on the other hand, had promised less and delivered more—much more—than I had expected. I had been the recipient of impeccable, personalized service from, in my mind, the most unlikely of service providers—a taxi cab driver!

The next morning I found myself standing before 65 franchise owners and managers of the sub sandwich company responsible for bringing me to Columbia in the first place. For almost three hours, we explored and discussed leadership and customer service strategy, along with practical service enhancement ideas.

Make The Ordinary Extraordinary

But our time together went too quickly for me. There was much more that I wanted to share. Much more that I wanted them to take away. With time slipping away, I became more intent on leaving the group with a challenge they could take home with them. However, nothing specific came to mind until I happened to glance at my watch. It was 11:40 a.m.

Only 20 minutes left. What can I do now that they will be sure to remember? Wait! That might work!

Before I had the time to think the entire illustration through, I heard myself saying the following.

"It's 11:40 a.m. Your stores have been open for about an hour to an hour and a half. How many of you can guarantee me that, right now, your staff is doing EXACTLY what they should be doing to satisfy and amaze your customers?"

I quickly surveyed the faces in the room for some definitive reaction. All I saw were blank looks. So I forged ahead into the unknown.

"For example, how many of you can guarantee me that each customer that visits your restaurant today will be greeted individually, warmly, and made to feel special and appreciated? How many of you can guarantee me that the food preparation line is stocked properly and is visually attractive so that every individual order can be filled as efficiently and as appealingly as possible? How many of you can guarantee me that your restrooms and dining areas are clean, orderly, and will be kept that way throughout the entire course of this shift and every shift to follow? How many of you can guarantee that these basic service expectations are being met and exceeded right now in your restaurants?"

The questions presented quite a challenge and I knew it. To the credit of those in attendance, they were thoughtful and honest in their responses. "I hope all those things are happening." "That's what we train them to do." "That's what we expect." . . . was the common sentiment among the group. But that wasn't enough for me. I wanted to drive the point home in a way that would be difficult for them to forget.

Willie's Way

Before I realized the scope of what I was about to say, these words spewed forth from my lips, "As the leaders of your businesses, it's your responsibility to make sure that your service expectations will be met! Your employees must know that you're counting on them to deliver professional service and that you have the ultimate confidence they will do so!"

Then, while still mounted on my proverbial soapbox, I finished my mini-rant with this outrageous statement. "I've got a plane to catch in a little while that will take me to Arizona. But, I can't catch it by myself. So I've already taken the time to ensure the service I need to make it to the airport on time. THEREFORE, I'LL BET ANYONE IN THIS ROOM ONE HUNDRED DOLLARS THAT MY CAB DRIVER WILL BE HERE AT 12 NOON SHARP!"

That was my first and only mention of my cab driver to this audience. They had no idea about my experience with him from the previous day. Furthermore, I had not planned to use the illustration and had not thought it through completely before issuing the challenge. I simply got caught up in the spirit of the moment. Nevertheless, the full magnitude of my comment hit me as I watched it register on the faces of my audience members.

WHAT HAVE I DONE? I CAN'T BELIEVE IT! I JUST BET $6,500... MY WIFE WILL KILL ME!!

So, I quickly added, "But if he shows up by noon, you've got to pay me my hundred dollars before you leave."

I admitted this was a foolish illustration and the group laughed it off with me, while I reemphasized the importance of shared expectations and commitment before moving on.

A few minutes later, at exactly four minutes before noon, something strange happened. I was just beginning my closing statements when six of the program participants got up and exited the room together. I couldn't imagine their reason for leaving with such a short time left in the program.

Make The Ordinary Extraordinary

Are they angry? Did I say something to upset them? Have they had all they can stand?

Not knowing what else to do, I simply forged ahead with my concluding remarks. Just before issuing my final "thank you" of the program—at 12 noon sharp—and exactly four minutes after their abrupt departure, the six program participants reappeared through the door in the back of the room. Once inside, they stood en masse, waiting to be recognized.

What now?

Unsure of what was to come, I cautiously asked, "Yes?"

With no further prompting, one of the six responded simply, "Your cab driver, Willie, is here!"

Gales of laughter reverberated through the room. Seeing my opening, I assumed a self-confident stance and responded with, "Well, I knew he would be!" More laughter followed.

It proved to be a wonderfully positive way to conclude the program. Afterwards, I milled around and talked with individual program participants for several minutes. One by one, they drifted away to lunch, at which point, I gathered my bags before making my way back to the lobby and out to my waiting cab.

As I exited the building, I saw Willie standing beside his cab, waiting for me. He was smiling. From 15 feet away, I still could see very little of his lips, but the creases and "smile lines" around his eyes were a dead giveaway.

"How you doing today, Willie?" I asked casually.

His response was succinct, to the point and to my way of thinking, priceless.

"Phil, ya been talkin' about me, ain't ya?"

Yeah, I was talking about Willie that day and have for many days since. I've been talking about Willie because of the valuable lessons of service I saw on display during my brief experience with this unassuming service professional.

In a broad sense, Willie showed me how his unique brand of personalized service can serve to "woo" (entice) customers to new and additional levels of business activity and involvement. It can "wow" (impress) customers whenever and wherever we come in contact with them. It can "win" (secure) customers by capturing their trust and confidence while building and sustaining profitable, long-term business relationships.

Just as important, I came to realize the attitude Willie possessed and the techniques he employed were available to any one of us who might truly be interested in learning and practicing them. This book is committed to helping people learn service professionalism, *Willie's Way*.

Secret # 1

Acknowledge Your Customers Immediately

*My name is William Watson.
My friends call me Willie. I'd appreciate it
if you'd call me Willie, too.*
— Willie Watson

Looking back, little did I know that as I begrudgingly made my way to the taxi cab waiting outside that South Carolina airport that my personal standard for measuring those who provide service to others would soon change. I was about to meet the man who would initiate that change and establish the new standard. But how could I have known? As far as I was concerned, this was just another cab ride. One of many. I expected the service experience to be more of the same.

Willie Watson, on the other hand, viewed this encounter far differently. Willie knew that if the service—and the attitude with which he offered it—were impressive enough, this encounter could be special. And if the encounter was special enough, the possibility existed that a positive economic benefit could result. Make no mistake about it. Willie Watson was a nice guy. But he was also an entrepreneur, a businessman. In Willie's business, better tips and additional business opportunities spelled the difference between profit and loss on a day-by-day, fare-by-fare basis.

Willie, therefore, had the upper hand in this service encounter. Even before the encounter took place, he knew what he needed to do to build a positive experience for the customer. He saw customers like me come and go every day. Over time, he had learned the importance of establishing a personal connection with his customers early on, in order to set the stage for the positive service experience to follow.

But Willie also knew that his window of opportunity was limited. If his passenger was able to make it to the back seat of his cab without that initial positive connection being made, there was a real possibility that the passenger might soon be engaged in a telephone conversation, have his faced buried in a newspaper, or even fall asleep, any of which would mean the opportunity for personal connection was lost, possibly forever.

Willie was unwilling to take that risk. He recognized that the first few seconds of any business encounter often set the stage, positively or negatively, for all that could follow. Rather than wishing and hoping, Willie was engaged in planning and acting. He put his plans into action by acknowledging me before I had even made it to his cab. ("Hey, buddy. Need a ride? I've been sittin' here waitin' for ya.") He then personalized the relationship even further once we were both inside the cab ("My name is William Watson. My friends call me Willie. I'd appreciate it if you'd call me Willie, too.")

With two master strokes, he accomplished what many who labor in service-related jobs never learn. First, he effortlessly broke down the invisible barrier between two strangers, the one in which one party waits uncomfortably for the other to speak or act. Second, he offered me the opportunity—the invitation—to be included in that elite group of individuals he calls his "friends." And he accomplished both with two well-planned and well-executed statements.

You may be wondering if the focused actions that Willie embraced are available only to entrepreneurial cab drivers, or if these techniques could benefit other professional service providers as well. The good news is that the techniques are available to anyone willing to learn and practice them. The sad news is that too few people ever do.

Acknowledge Your Customers Immediately

Consider some additional examples—good and bad—of other service providers and how their approach to servicing their customers might compare to Willie's.

What Is a Customer?

Several years ago my wife Susan and I were on vacation driving up the United States' eastern seaboard. Our trip took us all the way to the state of Maine in search of picturesque coastlines, fresh lobster, and a break from the stifling, late summer heat and humidity of our native South. As is our vacation custom, there were very few firmly established items on our travel agenda. But on one stop we had both agreed. We were determined to visit the anchor store for L.L.Bean, located in Freeport, Maine.

New Englanders have known about L.L.Bean for decades. But for many other North Americans, our knowledge has been limited to L.L.Bean's mail order catalogs. Personally, I had enjoyed their merchandise for years. Their sterling reputation for quality products and service—albeit almost always long distance service—was nothing short of legendary. But the hook for me was the claim the store made that they never closed. I had to see for myself.

Susan and I arrived at the L.L.Bean retail store shortly after 1:00 a.m. As one might imagine, there were few customers and only a smattering of staff to be found in the wee hours of the morning. Nevertheless, Susan was soon lost to me in her dogged pursuit of all things Gore-Tex, flannel, and fleece. Her absence allowed me the opportunity to wander the premises, exploring on my own.

As I sauntered up one aisle and down another, I eventually found myself in a back corner of the building. There I noticed something stenciled on the wall for all to see. As I drew closer and began to read, I soon found myself wondering if it had been placed there for the benefit of customers—or as a constant, very visible reminder to all L.L.Bean employees. It read:

At L.L.Bean a Customer Is . . .

- The most important person to us, whether in person, by phone or mail.
- Not dependent on us, but us on them.
- Not an interruption of our work, but our purpose for doing it.
- Human like us, with feelings, emotions and biases.
- Not someone to argue or match wits with.

The simple, straightforward message grabbed me. I thought it a good working example to share in my future customer training programs. So right there I took out my pen and began scribbling the words from the wall on a piece of scrap paper. Soon I was totally immersed in this solitary activity when someone suddenly tapped me on the shoulder. The physical touch startled me and caused me to jump. I had assumed I was all alone. I whirled and found myself face-to-face with a young store clerk who, seconds earlier, I didn't know existed.

"Excuse me, sir. I didn't mean to frighten you," he said sincerely. "I was just curious if there is a problem I can help you with?"

"No, I don't think so," I replied nervously, still working to regain my composure. "Why do you ask?"

"Well, sir, I couldn't help but notice that you were focused on our customer commitment statement," he said, pointing in the direction of the wall. "I just wanted to offer my assistance if you were experiencing any sort of problem."

I resisted the temptation to say what I was thinking. *You mean a problem other than almost causing me a heart attack?*

As I began to realize the sincerity of his motive, I moved from being startled to being thrilled.

Here is someone who gets it! He really gets it! Serving the needs of customers has become real to him.

Acknowledge Your Customers Immediately

Don't be fooled. One cannot determine a company's or an individual's true commitment to servicing their customers simply by some fancy, well-scripted proclamation printed on glossy paper, etched in granite, or even stenciled on a wall for all to see.

Willie Watson didn't have his service commitment monogrammed on his shirt. Willie didn't hire a public relations company to craft and promote his "service creed." No, Willie earned his service stripes the old-fashioned way by seeking out and servicing individual customers—whenever, wherever, and in whatever manner he could.

A true commitment to service is always mirrored in the actions of isolated professionals. Someone once said, "Character is what's on display when no one is watching." No one was watching Willie during our ride from the airport to the hotel. No one was watching this third shift L.L.Bean sales clerk. No one, that is, but me—the customer. And both of them responded marvelously. They met and exceeded my expectations.

Keep in mind the customer is always watching. It's either the customer you are interacting with presently or the one who is trying to determine if he or she wants to interact with you in the future. Do a good job and the customer will likely return again and again. Be indifferent to the customer who is watching, and the outcome most likely will mean opportunities lost.

Opportunities Lost

Too often, unfortunately, instead of the customer being acknowledged and appreciated immediately by the service provider, the customer is ignored and taken for granted. The business consequences of such shortsighted actions can be devastating.

Susan and I work together. She laughingly tells people that after 20 years of marriage, our personal and professional relationships still work because I travel and am gone much of the time.

Willie's Way

A few years ago, I was home for a stretch of several days. During that time, I was doing my best to try to lighten her load a bit, while at the same time earning some much-needed bonus points.

"Susan, how can I help you this morning? Do you need me to run any errands for you?" I asked.

"Well, I need to run by the bank and make a deposit, but it's really easier to do it myself," she responded.

"Don't be ridiculous," I countered. "I will be happy to go to the bank for you. Just tell me what you need me to do."

Hesitant at first, as if unsure of my overall ability to complete this simple task, Susan finally entrusted to me the business deposit. In addition, she included very specific instructions as to which of the branches of our nationally known bank I was to patronize. I listened carefully, in spite of being a bit insulted. Admittedly, Susan did most of our banking transactions. *But, really. How hard can this little project be?*

Per Susan's instructions, I drove to the bank's branch office nearest our home. I pulled into the lot and drove past the bank's stylish sign, manicured lawn, and modern building, straight to the convenient "customer-friendly" drive-through canopy. There were five lanes in operation. I noticed that lane number three was unoccupied, so I pulled my vehicle into the lane and rolled to a stop beside the "automatic teller." I rolled down my window and paused briefly. I heard nothing. I noticed an empty cylinder lying in its cradle beside me. I retrieved the cylinder, inserted my deposit and returned the cylinder to the cradle. Still no sounds. Upon closer inspection, I noticed a green "SEND" button. I pushed the button. With a great sucking sound, the cylinder and my deposit were whisked away into nothing-ness. I sat briefly in total silence. Not more than two minutes later, a loud whooshing sound announced the re-emergence of the cylinder, this time containing a receipt where my deposit had previously been. I collected the receipt from the cylinder and returned the cylinder to its holder. I sat for a moment longer, listening to more silence.

Acknowledge Your Customers Immediately

Finally, I rolled up the window and pulled away, headed for home. The entire experience had lasted less than three minutes. My transaction was apparently handled correctly and with unquestioned efficiency. Yet, the brief experience left me feeling cold and ambivalent.

"Did you go to the bank?" Susan asked upon my return.

"Of course, I did. Here's the receipt."

"Any problems?"

"Not really," I said haltingly. "But one thing kind of bothered me."

"What's that?" Susan asked.

"Well, I used the drive-through like you suggested. But, throughout the entire transaction, no one inside the building spoke to me. Not a single word. I thought that was strange."

"Phil, I drive through there all the time. They never speak," Susan said simply, never looking up.

At first I was amazed, then irritated. How could the act of customer service have gotten so routine, so mechanized, so impersonal that organizations no longer see the need to acknowledge the customer?

Surely, we're both missing something, I thought. I need to see for myself.

For the next two days I insisted on making the "bank run." Sadly, I discovered Susan was right. I did business in the same lane at the same bank branch for three days in a row and not once did I ever hear a human voice. Not "Good morning," "Thank you," "Kiss my foot," nothing! I admit the transactions were processed correctly each time and there was very little waiting. But with each unacknowledged visit, I became more and more annoyed until finally I announced my intention to close our accounts and place our meager funds in some other more customer-friendly financial institution. Susan had her doubts, but I insisted.

Willie's Way

The next day we closed our accounts and withdrew our money with absolutely no fanfare. I didn't expect our decision to make front page news in the *Wall Street Journal*. I didn't expect them to bar the doors and throw themselves in our path to keep us from leaving. I didn't expect there to be crying and gnashing of teeth at the news of our decision. I did, however, expect someone at the bank to be trained to ask us one little question: "Why?" But, once again, my most basic of expectations simply went unmet. Instead, the bank representative simply processed our final request (very efficiently, I might add) and watched us walk out their door forever.

Do you not realize that with us goes your last chance to lend us money for cars, motorcycles, vacations, home and office remodeling, business expansion projects, and three—count 'em—three upcoming college educations? Do you not realize you will never again earn fees from checks we write, our visits to the ATM machine, and various other personal services that you offer? Don't you understand that our three children will one day need a financial institution of their own, and based on our recommendation, you're not going to be it? Can you really afford to disassociate yourself so easily and thoughtlessly from established customers like us?

The thought of any business being so callused toward their customer base that they show no interest or obvious concern in knowing why their customers are leaving is simply flabbergasting to me.

I wish I could tell you that exhaustive research and extensive interviews with various bank officers, managers, and staff led us to choose our next financial services supplier. I wish I could tell you that we knew exactly what our new bank offered in terms of personalized financial services. I wish I could tell you I knew how our new bank ranked on key financial measurements compared to other available local, state, regional, and national banks. I wish I could tell you I knew those things before selecting our new bank. But it wouldn't be the truth. In fact, I believe very few people take the time to research banks, credit unions, accounting practices, law firms, brokerage houses,

Acknowledge Your Customers Immediately

automobile dealerships, realty companies, restaurants, department stores, barbers, and hairdressers *before* they begin doing business with them. I am convinced most initial business relationships begin with a "gut feel." A gut feel assures us somehow that we will enjoy doing business with the *people* who represent the business.

I must admit that I chose our next bank very *unscientifically*. It wasn't the bank that was nearest our home and office. In fact, it was more inconvenient than our previous bank. It wasn't the bank that had the most financial options available. Frankly, I never asked what was available. I chose the bank because of one person I knew at the bank—plain and simple. One of the bank's branch managers, Mark, and I had served on a local committee together. I didn't know Mark well, but he had always been friendly and outgoing. I liked the way he treated me and others with whom I saw him interacting. That was enough for me.

"Phil, it's good to see you. What can I do for you this morning?" Mark asked.

"I am here to open both a business account and a personal account," I stated flatly.

"Fantastic! We love new customers," he responded enthusiastically, as he began gathering the necessary forms and paperwork.

"Not so fast, Mark. I intend to open those accounts. But *first* I want to tell you exactly *why* I left my last bank."

"Of course, Phil," Mark responded, obviously confused. "I would love to know why you were unhappy with your last bank."

"Because they wouldn't speak to me, Mark. I drove through their drive-through teller line three days in a row and no one ever spoke a word to me. That bothered me. That bothered me a lot. Mark, do you understand what I'm telling you?"

"Perfectly, Phil," Mark assured me.

From that day forth, until we finally moved out of the area years later, I could not walk into the lobby of that branch without a half dozen employees greeting me personally and enthusiastically. "Good morning, Mr. Van Hooser." "How are you today, Mr. Van Hooser?" "Beautiful day, isn't it, Mr. Van Hooser?"

I know what you're wondering.

Does Phil recognize Mark had probably coached his employees to respond to him in that specific way? Of course, I recognize it. Any bright manager would instruct his employees to do what they could to meet and exceed the known expectations of their customers. To do less would be foolish, or worse, arrogant. When professional arrogance serves to discount the customer's role in the company's success, that's the first step toward committing professional, or economic, suicide.

Did the fact these employees were coached lessen the spontaneity, genuineness, or impact of the experience for Phil? Absolutely not. Let's face it. We all have to *learn* to do our jobs. If we learn to offer service incorrectly, or if we have never been trained properly to offer quality, personal service in the first place, then at some point we have to relearn the activity. Spontaneity, genuineness, and impact happen once we learn the basics of a service activity and then start to insert our own personality from there. I loved the recognition, acknowledgment, and relationship building regular visits to the bank afforded me.

Or maybe you're thinking something along these lines.

For some reason, Phil must think he deserves special treatment. Exactly! I do think I deserve special treatment by every person with whom I do business. Why? Is it because I think I'm better than someone else? Absolutely not. I appreciate special treatment when I experience it because I know it means someone has taken the time to think about me, their customer. They care about how I feel. When that happens, it makes me want to do more business with such caring and attentive people.

Acknowledge Your Customers Immediately

But Phil, does it bother you to know that Mark is coaching his employees to treat all the bank's customers the same way they are treating you? Heavens, no! It would have confirmed what I already believed—that Mark understood the game of business.

Mark had, in his own way, captured the essence of what it means to offer service "Willie's Way." Willie Watson understood the necessity of making customers feel special. He understood how the game of service is played.

The Game of Service Is the Game of Business

"Is business a game?" you ask. "It can't be. Business is serious . . . well . . . business!"

Okay, I agree. Business is serious. There's a lot riding on the outcome. But think just a moment of the game of business in the same terms as you would any other competitive game in which you enjoy participating, such as tennis, chess, or Monopoly. Each of these games shares a number of common characteristics. For example, each is governed by a specific set of rules. The rules are usually fairly easy to understand, but not always easy to follow. Each game requires players to be pitted against at least one other opponent. Finally, for a positive outcome to be realized, either or both participants must possess the skill and strategy to accomplish their individual goals.

The "individual goals" of both parties are where things begin to get sticky. In tennis, chess, or Monopoly the goal is to beat the opponent as soundly as possible. However, in the game of business, to be really successful—to be a truly expert player—both parties must win the first time and every time thereafter. For example, those who provide products and services must make their customers happy by providing quality products and services at a reasonable price, while still making a necessary profit. But they can't just do it once and be forever satisfied. One profitable business exchange does not a successful business make. Sustainable businesses have been and always will be built on the foundation of repeat business.

Willie's Way

Successful automobile dealers prosper when their customers return every three or four years in search of their next vehicle. Restaurateurs prosper when their patrons establish a habit of eating with them regularly. Barbers and hairdressers prosper when their customers return to their chairs every few weeks, without once thinking about where else they might be able to get their hair cut or styled.

In business, like in other games, there are certain to be winners and losers. Each is fairly easy to spot. The winners are the ones sporting the logos on the side of their trucks that proclaim "Doing business since 1957," or "Voted #1 for the eleventh year in a row." The winners are the ones who continue to expand their product lines and service offerings. The winners are the ones who report sustained growth and profitability quarter after quarter, year after year. The winners are the ones who have the best and brightest talent clamoring to join their ranks.

But the losers in the game of business are easy to spot, too. The losers are the ones who place "GOING OUT OF BUSINESS" signs in the storefront windows. The losers are the ones acting as if business in the twenty-first century will be the same as it was in the twentieth century. The losers are the ones filing for bankruptcy, or worse, doctoring their own books to mislead others. The losers are the ones who vigorously contest every customer complaint. The losers are the ones who undercut the authority and ability of their own employees to handle customer complaints directly.

I'm not suggesting every successful business is successful solely because of its service expertise, or that every unsuccessful business is struggling solely because of a lack of service focus. The game of business is much more complicated than that. But I do believe those who prosper in the game of business are those who take the time to learn the game in the first place. And in learning the game, it is impossible to discount the importance of having satisfied customers who continue to do business with us and who are willing to share a goodwill message with others about us and the products and services we offer. Whether the business is distributing hundreds of bottles of barbecue

Acknowledge Your Customers Immediately

sauce locally or overseeing millions of dollars of Medicare reimbursements nationwide, whether the business is intent on rebuilding your automobile's engine or giving your spine an adjustment, one thing is for sure—it's all about the customer.

He'll Know My Name

I hadn't been in Willie's cab for more than 30 seconds before he had already introduced himself to me and learned my name. During the next 30 minutes or so, Willie used my name in casual conversation at least two dozen times. And it was all so natural. After our first few minutes together, I consciously forgot that our relationship was that of customer and service provider. It came to feel more like a discussion between friends. Therein rests the magic and the power of using a customer's name. People are drawn together.

Of course, customers are not just those individuals walking into our showroom or calling us on the telephone. Those customers tend to get our immediate attention. Their faces are not as familiar to us. They come from outside the company. We refer to them as our *external* customers.

But we should never discount the importance of our *internal* customers as well. Most of us have them. Internal customers are our co-workers, with whom we interact daily, as we strive to serve the needs of the external customers.

Unfortunately, because our internal customers have become so familiar to us over time, like our own family members, too often we end up taking them for granted. The critical need to acknowledge our *internal* customers and their contributions cannot be overstated. When working with my corporate clients, I often remind them that if they improve their internal customer service activities, their external customers will benefit from it. If not, it is hard to predict exactly what problems will ensue.

Years ago, I was working as a Human Resources Manager in a nonunion manufacturing facility. During my time there, a union organizing drive was initiated by a relatively small, but determined group of employees. Day after day, for several weeks, this group actively solicited their fellow employees in hopes of gaining support for their labor union of choice.

One of the more vocal internal supporters of this movement was a middle-aged machine operator whom I will call "Lonnie." I remember Lonnie specifically for two reasons. First, I remember his involvement with this organizing group as being totally out of character for him. In the four years I had worked with Lonnie, I had found him to be intelligent, capable, and a hard worker, but very quiet, reserved, and inclined to remain in the background regarding public issues. He had stressed to me a number of times over the years that he preferred not to speak out in public and that he didn't enjoy taking on leadership roles. Yet, there he was, not only speaking out, but leading the charge.

The second reason I remember him so well is because of something Lonnie once said to me. I had always seen my role of Human Resources Manager as a type of local liaison, or go-to person, for both labor and management. As such, I spent a good portion of every workday interacting with production employees on the shop floor, as well as with management people in the front office.

One day, while walking through the plant, Lonnie whistled to get my attention and then motioned for me to join him at his work station. I made my way to him to see what was on his mind. He was quick to let me know.

"Phil, I haven't had the chance to tell you this before, but I wanted you to know that my involvement in this union drive has nothing to do with you personally. I appreciate what you do to help address some of the issues that are a concern to us," Lonnie said quietly, with sincerity in his voice. It was something he didn't have to tell me, especially during a time of heightened tensions in the company.

"Thanks for saying so, Lonnie. I appreciate hearing that from you."

It could be argued that I would have been better off stopping right there. But, Lonnie had initiated this conversation, not me. Now there was something I really wanted to know. And the best way to find out was to ask.

Acknowledge Your Customers Immediately

"This is really none of my business and it won't hurt my feelings if you choose not to answer. But, I'm curious. Lonnie, why are you so involved in this union movement? This is really not like you."

Lonnie's eyes were quick to lock on mine. I watched as his quiet demeanor changed right before me. In mere seconds, he stopped being quiet and unassuming. In a moment of transformation, he became determined and outspoken.

"Phil, I have worked at this plant for nine years. I have done almost every job in this department. I have worked all three shifts and Lord only knows how many hours of overtime," he said. Then he paused briefly and pointed across the plant in the direction of the plant manager who stood talking with another employee.

"Phil, do you see that man right there?" he asked, his voice brimming with resentment. "After all these years, he doesn't even know my name. I dare you to call him over right now and ask him to tell you my name. I guarantee you he wouldn't be able to do it. Can you believe that? After nine years of working together, he still doesn't know my name!" Then Lonnie paused for another moment as his eyes returned and fixed themselves on mine. Then he added, "But, when this is all over, he'll know my name."

Putting It Into Practice

Willie Watson taught me that the principle of acknowledgment is universal. Whether it's an L.L.Bean salesclerk, some anonymous bank teller or a plant manager in some manufacturing facility, the need to acknowledge our customers immediately and regularly—whether they are with us for five minutes a month or eight hours every day—is the critical first step to "wooing," "wowing," and "winning" customers and the loyalty they have to share.

Here are three suggestions to help you acknowledge your customers more professionally:

1. Move to the customer or at least make eye contact as soon as possible.

It is important to physically move to the customer. Never wait for the customer to come to you. The sooner you approach the customer, the less time you allow the customer to formulate mental obstacles, objections, or negative impressions that could adversely affect his or her interest in interacting or doing business with you. If you are temporarily unable to move to the customer (i.e., you are on the phone or helping someone else), make every effort to use some form of facial expression or body language to acknowledge the customer and let them know they are important to you.

2. Introduce yourself to unfamiliar customers (internal or external) immediately.

"Hi, my name is Phil. I don't believe we've met. What's your name?"

Never expect the customer to speak first. To hesitate, even briefly, may make you appear aloof, pretentious, or unapproachable in the eyes of the customer—all of which are avoidable barriers if you introduce yourself first. Remember, the most important name in any introduction is not yours.

3. Once you know the customer's name, repeat it at as often as possible during your conversation.

"Mr. Smith, it's nice to meet you."

"Is there something special I can help you with today, Mr. Smith?"

"Mr. Smith do you live or work in the area?"

"How did you learn about the services we offer, Mr. Smith?"

"I appreciate you stopping by today, Mr. Smith. Here's my card, please call me directly if I can be of further service to you."

Acknowledge Your Customers Immediately

"Thank you, Mr. Smith. I look forward to seeing you again."

Notice that each of these sentences could have easily been asked without using Mr. Smith's name. However, using the customer's name repeatedly helps solidify the name in your mind as you build on this and future service opportunities. Hearing his name also makes the service experience more personal for the customer.

Secret # 2

Redefine Your Routine Activities

*You're my first customer today, Phil.
I've been sittin' in that line waitin' for ya.*
– Willie Watson

For good or for bad, routines rule our lives.

Whether you've considered it or not, we all have routines—or in too many cases, routines have us. Many of the routines we follow were initiated after careful thought, meticulous planning, and conscientious implementation. We embrace such routines for a simple reason—they work for us.

Other routines have, over time, slipped insidiously into the fabric of our lives without our permission and possibly without our conscious knowledge. They were not built after careful thought and planning, although they have become so ingrained, we feel almost powerless to rid ourselves of them.

Positive routines can change your life, your work and your relationships for the better. They truly can help make you healthier, wealthier, and wise. On the contrary, negative routines can sabotage and undercut your personal and professional efforts to such a degree that your life, work, and even relationships can be damaged, sometimes irreparably.

Willie Watson was not immune to such considerations. Like all of us, his life was full of routines. It is safe to say that as a cab driver, Willie routinely worked long hours for minimal compensation. His work routine brought him into regular contact with passengers who were impatient, angry, sick, confused, frustrated, in a hurry, and occasionally, even dangerous. Under such circumstances, it would not have been unusual or unheard of to learn that Willie had adopted complementary routines to help him deal with such attitudes. He could have become withdrawn, aggressive, sullen, whiny, overbearing, suspicious, or intolerant.

However, by his actions that I witnessed, it is obvious to me Willie opted to manage his routines rather than allowing his routines to manage him. Instead of sitting in his cab for hours on end sulking, going over and over in his mind the negatives associated with his work, Willie preferred to focus on the possibilities, not the problems. Willie made sure his mind was occupied with thoughts and ideas that would help ensure positive experiences for the passengers he would encounter that day, which in turn could mean a better financial outcome for himself.

At their best, the positive routines we adopt in our jobs can serve as a foundation of customer confidence from which we can continue to build ever-more impressive service activities. For example, if we develop the routine of answering each business call before the third ring, our regular customers soon equate that routine with the perception that we are committed to promptness and consistency in all of our service activities. If we respond to each phone message and e-mail received before the end of the business day, our customers come to expect that communication problems with us will be minimal or nonexistent.

At their worst, the routine activities in our jobs can lead us to be lackadaisical, bored, and unresponsive in our attitudes and ultimately, in the service we offer. If we are slow to answer incoming calls or prone to leave customers on hold for prolonged periods, over time we create the impression of being unprofessional or worse, unconcerned about the needs of our customers. If we are haphazard in the way we respond to calls and e-mails, customers may eventually opt to do business with individuals they can connect and communicate with more easily.

Willie Watson knew the importance of taking care of the "little things" related to customer service and satisfaction. Little things like personal connection, common courtesy, and the importance of establishing positive routines. When the little things are taken care of, the big things have a way of taking care of themselves. However, if we ignore or overlook those little things, too often they grow and fester over time, becoming the "big things" that can destroy customer confidence and ultimately a business relationship.

Finishing School for Motorcycle Cops

The phone rang in my office. I recognized the voice on the other end of the line even before he identified himself.

"Phil, this is Randy. I need some help."

Randy was a long-time client. More specifically, he was the officer in charge of training for one of the larger law enforcement agencies in the Southeast. Over a period of several years, Randy had hired me on a number of occasions to create and present internal leadership training programs for various groups of officers throughout his agency. We had always worked well together and had become friends. Our relationship had a special quality, in that the trust level had been developed to the degree that we felt comfortable shooting straight with one another. I was glad to hear from him. But he sounded troubled.

"Randy, it's good to hear your voice. What's going on?"

"I just came out of a meeting with the agency's chief of staff. He was not happy. It seems he recently received the results of some number crunching that has been going on at the highest levels in the organization. During the past six months, well over 90 percent of all the citizen complaints the agency has received have been directed toward our motorcycle traffic patrol division. Most of the complaints center around little aggravations alleging the officer was unnecessarily rude or uncommunicative during routine traffic stops. Phil, it's bad enough to get a ticket. It's worse still if the motorist leaves feeling as if he or she has been talked down to or belittled. Anyway, because of the complaints, my boss is getting heat from his boss—so now I'm getting heat, too. He expects me to do something to fix this problem—and soon."

"Randy, I'm sorry to hear that, but what does that have to do with me?"

"Phil, I need your help. Do you think you can you create a finishing school for motorcycle cops?"

A "finishing school?" That reminds me of the old days when genteel young ladies were sent away to learn the finer points of how to walk, how to talk, and how to drink tea with their pinky fingers extended. Somehow that was supposed to ensure that they became respectable young women.

When I think of motorcycle cops I think of the old C.H.I.P.S. television show. Huge men, muscles bulging through polyester uniforms, wearing knee-high leather boots, mirrored sunglasses, and straddling a big Harley Davidson motorcycle.

I appreciated the contrast in images.

"Randy, are you serious?" I chuckled.

"Phil, I'm dead serious. If we can create a training program that will make our officers aware of the importance of good old, garden variety manners, then our efforts can make an immediate and positive impact on how our agency is viewed by citizens. Beyond that, maybe it will even help break down some of the stereotypical attitudes people have about cops in general and motorcycle cops in particular. This is a training program unlike any we have ever offered before. You will be plowing new ground. I see it as a wonderful opportunity for you to really make a difference through your work."

Randy was a good salesman. His words made sense. This was an opportunity to make a difference. The more we talked, the more the opportunity excited me. Eventually, I accepted the challenge and began the process of creating a six-hour customer-service training program customized specifically for motorcycle patrol officers.

Redefine Your Routine Activities

The day for the scheduled training finally arrived. As was my custom, I met and greeted each of the participants as they entered the training room. I was excited. Randy seemed excited. But it soon became clear that 35 motorcycle cops didn't share our excitement. One in particular sent a very clear message upon his arrival.

"Good morning," I offered as he walked in.

"What's so [expletive deleted] good about it?" he growled loudly, as he brushed past me on the way to an open seat in the back of the room. Upon hearing his comment, some of his colleagues laughed openly.

Oh, great. It's going to be one of those kind of groups.

With the realization of the challenge before me, I prepared myself mentally and emotionally as best I could.

Once the group was assembled, Randy turned to me and said, "Phil, I'll start by saying a few words about why we're here today and then I'll introduce you, okay?"

"Sounds fine to me."

The following is EXACTLY how Randy started the program and how I was introduced that day. Randy strode to the front of the room and faced the unappreciative group. He apparently had decided the direct approach was the best approach.

"All right, listen up," he began gruffly. "Y'all know why we're here. There's no sense beating around the bush. Your customer service stinks! Citizens are calling and complaining about this group constantly. Management spends 90 percent of their time trying to fix what y'all have screwed up," he said, his voice rising noticeably.

Thanks loads, Randy. There's nothing like a nice warm welcome to get a training program off on the right foot. Maybe you'd like to rub a little more salt in their wounds.

That's exactly what he did.

"Well, we're gonna fix this problem today, once and for all. Understand?" he continued menacingly. "We've brought this guy in from out of town and we're paying him a lot of money to be here, so pay attention!" Randy then turned toward me and said, "Phil, go ahead. They're all yours."

All mine? I'm not sure I want them now! I thought.

I took a deep breath and stepped to the front of the coldest room I can ever remember. Thirty-five sets of steely eyes glared at me. Most had removed their mirrored sunglasses. It might have been better if they hadn't.

Well, here I go. What have I got to lose? What's the worst thing that can happen anyway? If they don't like what I have to say, they're not going to shoot me.

At that very moment, I glanced around the room and came to a startling realization. I was the *only* unarmed person in the room.

Oh, well, so much for that theory! Maybe if I keep moving around the room I'll be harder to hit.

With my sense of humor and optimism still partially intact, for the next hour and a half I gave it my all. I imparted every service statistic I could conjure up. I shared every conceivable service story and illustration that could be applied to law enforcement. I employed every participative training technique I had ever learned. Nothing worked. Absolutely nothing. This group was hardcore. They had convinced themselves this topic was irrelevant to their jobs. Their body language and snide remarks communicated the attitude: "We're cops, not store clerks. Come back when you have something that relates to us." As a result, the training program was going nowhere—fast. The group was totally unresponsive. They weren't willing to see the connection. As for me, I couldn't help but see the clock.

Just 90 minutes gone? I've still got four and a half hours to go! That's an eternity. This is torture. I've got to do something different.

Redefine Your Routine Activities

I looked toward the back of the room and noticed the officer who had greeted me so rudely and crudely earlier. He sat with his beefy arms crossed over his burly chest. He had pushed himself away from his table and was sitting in a "reclined" position with his long legs extended and crossed in front of him and his head thrown back. The program handout I had prepared lay untouched before him, where it had been placed more than two hours earlier. Like the others, he glared straight back at me.

This one is as good as any. No guts, no glory!

"You're not buying any of this, are you?" I asked the officer directly.

"Not a bit," he responded confidently, without hesitation. "I think my customer service is just fine. I've been doing this for over 10 years. Why should I change now?"

"That's a good question. Now, let me ask you one. How many traffic stops will you make in an average day while working traffic patrol?"

The specificity of the question seemed to catch him off guard. I used his momentary hesitation as an opportunity to drive my point home.

"Don't try to impress me," I continued, adopting a no-nonsense tone to match the one he was using. "Your fellow officers will know if you're lying anyway. And don't tell me that the number of stops you make each day depends on a lot of different factors. I know that. I just want to know, on average—week in, week out—how many traffic stops you expect to make in a given day."

By now, the rest of the officers in the audience had perked up. Some had turned around completely in their seats to face their colleague. Others sat still, their eyes riveted on me, reading my body language. They realized something had changed. This was no longer a routine training activity. They sensed a confrontation brewing. They waited anxiously for their fellow officer's answer, if for no other reason than to see what would happen next.

"Well, there are some days when there are more. But on average, I guess I make about 10 stops a day," he said, somewhat tentatively.

I turned to the rest of the class for confirmation and involvement. "Is that a fair number? Is that about the same for all of you?" Most nodded in agreement and then sat back waiting for my response. I returned my attention to my original combatant.

"So let me get this straight. You make about 10 traffic stops a day. Since you work five days a week, it's fair to assume you make about 50 traffic stops each week. Is that right?"

"Yeah, I guess," he offered, still unsure of my intent.

"If you're making 50 traffic stops each week and you work about 50 weeks each year, it's safe to assume you're making somewhere around 2,500 traffic stops each year. Right?"

"So?" he asked suspiciously.

"Well, you said a minute ago that you've been doing this for more than 10 years. I figure, if you're making 2,500 traffic stops a year and you've been doing that for more than 10 years, then you've made in excess of 25,000 traffic stops in your career. Would you agree with my numbers?"

It was obvious the magnitude of the numbers impressed not only him, but all of the officers in the room. Apparently, none of them had ever taken the time to do this type of practical math before. As they sat mulling over the huge number, I asked the most important question.

"Now is it not fair to assume that after 25,000 traffic stops maybe your professional routine today is not as customer focused as it was after the 25th, 250th, or 2,500th stop? Is it possible that you've become a little bored or lackadaisical in the way you approach your job? Is it possible you take a few more shortcuts now than you used to? Is it possible that every now and then, you have been guilty of taking the motorists' feelings and unique situations for granted? Is it possible that you've grown tired of hearing the same old sob story every time you make a traffic stop? Is it possible that after all these years, you've become jaded and that your cynicism occasionally shows itself in your

Redefine Your Routine Activities

work? If so, is it possible there could be a few things—simple things—that you used to do to prove your professionalism to motorists that could be done again, that motorists—your customers—would appreciate more?"

To his credit, the officer reluctantly agreed.

"Well, that's what I'm here to help you do," I concluded, as we refocused on the practical aspects of service professionalism.

It was not my favorite training day of all time, but that experience with those motorcycle cops taught me a valuable lesson. By simply changing my training routine, I was eventually able to get this particular group to honestly re-examine their daily professional routines. In so doing, they recognized specific activities that could be improved that in turn could improve the experience of the "customers" they came into contact with. Yes, that's right. The recipients of tickets are in fact the customers of these officers.

Take a minute to consider all the routine things you do on a regular basis in your job and how long you've been doing them. You might be amazed at just how many sales calls you've made, how many letters you've sent, how many complaints you've dealt with, and how many conversations you've been involved in over the past 2, 5, 10, 20, or more years of professional activity. Now ask yourself honestly, are there specific actions I could take to improve each interaction somewhat? If so, can I legitimately expect to see the service I offer through these professional activities improve noticeably?

I am confident Willie Watson has ferried thousands of passengers to their desired destinations over the years. And I'm sure the limited amount of time he has to spend with each passenger makes it difficult to create a positive lasting impression with each one. In such a situation, Willie and others have found that even small changes in routine, if implemented flawlessly, can yield big service satisfaction results.

Consider another service professional, like Willie, who labors in relative anonymity but who is able to make a big difference in the attitudes of those he serves, in large part because his routine is focused and unique.

Willie's Way

A Service Pro at Work in Terminal A

For the better part of the past 20 years, my professional life has revolved around almost constant travel. I have spoken in hundreds of cities throughout North America. I have traveled through virtually every major airport in the United States and Canada, as well as dozens of smaller ones nestled throughout the countryside. I shudder to think how many airport meals I have consumed over the years. My number one airport for total flight segments—and calories consumed—is Atlanta's Hartsfield International Airport.

The Atlanta airport offers weary travelers literally dozens of culinary options, including snack machines, specialty kiosks, fast-food outlets, grills, and even "up-scale, sit-down" type venues. Everyone has his or her own personal preference. But, over time, I have determined what constitutes an acceptable airport meal for me: large portions, good quality, and reasonable prices.

You might wonder why good service is not included in my list of criteria. The main reason is practicality. I have discovered that if one is fortunate enough to actually find anything that remotely resembles "service" in an airport eatery these days—it's usually bad. Therefore, as a coping mechanism, I have found that if I don't expect much in the way of airport food service, I'm not nearly as disappointed when good service is not forthcoming. Strange as it may sound, this philosophy of embracing embarrassingly low expectations of airport food service works for me. However, occasionally I get pleasantly surprised.

I was traveling through the Atlanta airport around mealtime with about 90 minutes to spare before my next flight. As I stepped off the escalator, I found myself on the fringes of the Terminal A food court. *I've got a few minutes. This place is as good as any,* I thought as I maneuvered my way through the bustling crowd and positioned myself in one of the serving lines.

As we inched forward, I tried to keep my rolling travel case close beside me. My constant companion and life line on the road, this case was bulky enough to be a tripping hazard for unsuspecting pedestrians. Soon someone was

Redefine Your Routine Activities

shouting questions in my direction and I was shouting my order back to her. In seconds, an industrial-sized tray was thrust my way, on which was precariously balanced my supper. From the moment the tray touched my hand, an impromptu circus act ensued with me being the principal performer. I worked to balance the tray of food in one hand, retrieve my wallet with the other, while pushing my rolling case toward the cash register with my knees, all the while bumping and dodging other diners who found themselves in a similar predicament. It was a disaster waiting to happen.

When I finally reached the cash register, I vaguely heard a voice over my shoulder say, "I'll take that for you." Out of curiosity, I turned just in time to watch with shock and anger as a man—a total stranger—dragged my case away.

Could it be? Is this guy bold enough—or stupid enough—to steal my case in broad daylight? Should I shout for him to stop? Should I drop my food and chase after him?

My mind raced as I worked to process the unexpected images unfolding before me. Thankfully, before I overreacted and made a fool of myself, the stranger stopped beside one of the few empty tables, slid my case under the table, turned my way, and smiled broadly as he waited for me to come to him. I was still confused. I collected my receipt and change, along with the tray of food, and made my way suspiciously toward the man, the table, and my bag.

As I drew near, the gentleman produced a towel from his back pocket and with a great flourish, wiped the crumbs from the table before pulling my chair out for me. Before I could say a word, he smiled and said, "Sir, enjoy your meal," and walked away. I couldn't believe my eyes.

Am I hallucinating? Could it really be true? Was this stranger actually helping me?

It took a total of 13 minutes for me to eat my meal. I sat mesmerized for another 14 minutes watching this gentleman repeat his earlier performance with several more unsuspecting patrons like me. The results were always the same—looks of sheer amazement. Several times while I sat watching, this energetic customer servant, knowing that the spotlight was on him, would look my way and subtly smile, nod, or wink. He knew I was watching. And he knew he was special.

When I could delay no longer, I motioned for the young man.

"Sir, is there something else I can do for you?" he asked sincerely.

"No, you've done great. I just wanted you to know how impressed I am with your attitude and service. I don't see conscientious folks like you very often working in airports," I said, as I slipped him a tip. It was the first time I could ever remember tipping a food court worker. But then again, it was the first time I ever saw a food court worker do anything deserving of a tip.

"Why thank you, sir," he said, as he took the money and slipped it into his pocket. He then smiled and made his way back into the mass of humanity in search of others to serve.

What intrigued me so much about this young man's level of service? Why was I so impressed? Was it just because he was friendly and polite? Was it the fact that he actually wiped down my table and pulled out my chair for me?

It was all those things and more. This young man took a page from Willie Watson's personalized approach to customer service. He did something that literally anyone in a similar position *could have* done, yet in actually doing it, people found it to be unexpected. In short, he redefined the routine activities of greeting and seating patrons and of wiping down tables. He stepped out of the established, expected routine and inserted a bit of personality, creativity, and flair. As a result, he benefited financially from the tip I offered and from the tips of others.

Whether it's a cab driver in Columbia, South Carolina, or a custodial support person in Atlanta, Georgia, exceptional service professionals willing to alter their service routines to benefit the customer always stand out in a crowd. It works for companies, too.

Redefine Your Routine Activities

The 999 Drill

Individuals are not the only ones that get locked into routines. Organizations can as well. Yet, creative organizations are constantly trying to tweak their service activities, culture, and the perception their customers have of them. They recognize that in order to gain a competitive advantage, they must differentiate themselves in the eyes of their customers from the very beginning of the professional relationship.

At the corporate headquarters of Computer Services, Inc. (CSI), they do just that. CSI designs, develops, sells, and supports hardware and software account-processing services for community banks located all over the United States. Bank presidents, and financial services executives from all over America are common visitors in the lobby of CSI's impressive corporate headquarters in Paducah, Kentucky. Such guests generally expect to be welcomed warmly by the receptionist as they sign the visitors' log upon their arrival. However, first-time visitors don't expect what happens next at CSI.

Once these visiting dignitaries have logged in, the receptionist assures them that whomever they are there to see will be down to receive them shortly. The guests are greeted and escorted into CSI's Corporate Conference Room. It is then that the "999 call" goes out.

Over the internal paging system, the receptionist announces, "Steve Powless, dial 999. Steve Powless, please dial 999."

To the visitors and the uninitiated, the page seems innocuous enough. Hundreds of similar pages are heard in business offices across this country every day. But to the customer-service-minded professionals in CSI's headquarters, the "999 drill" is nothing short of a call to action.

You see, Steve Powless is CSI's president and CEO. But 999 is not Steve's office extension number. Neither is it the switchboard extension. In fact, there is no 999 extension on CSI's entire phone system. The page is nothing more than a predetermined code that signals all CSI corporate officers that important visitors are on the premises. When sounded, executives from all

49

over the building drop what they are doing and quickly make their way to the lobby area outside the conference room. In no more than two or three minutes, all on-site executives are present and accounted for. It is then the door to the conference room opens and in marches 10, 15, even 20 of CSI's top executives, management staff, and often, the company founder himself. Together, they warmly greet and welcome their guests, provide a brief overview of their area of responsibility, and finally thank each guest for coming to visit.

It's an impressive display to witness. It is even more impressive to be the recipient of such attention and honor. It's one of those experiences that sticks with you long after the occasion itself has passed. Why? Because it is out of the ordinary—it is not routine. Does this simple, but focused activity assure that the parties will always end up working together? Of course not. But, it does tend to make an indelible impression in the minds of those on which such attention is lavished. Why? Because it is unusual—out of the ordinary.

Putting It Into Practice

Regardless of the arena in which we offer service to our customers, there will be occasions when we find ourselves mired in the mundane, often mindless, routines of the jobs we have chosen. Take heart. All is not lost. If we will just take a few minutes to redefine the routine activities in our jobs, we may discover countless opportunities to prove our professionalism to our customers again and again.

Here are three practical suggestions to help you redefine your routine activities:

1. Take five minutes and write down which of the specific routines in your job you dread or dislike the most and would like to change.

Be honest with yourself. The first step to successfully managing any problem is to specifically identify that problem. Your dreaded routines may include the weekly staff meeting, the quarterly inventory, the annual customer review or others.

Redefine Your Routine Activities

2. Contact the most creative, imaginative person you know.

This person may be either a personal or professional friend or contact. Remember: It is not necessary that this person understands or has personal experience with each of the routines you have identified. Call the person and ask to buy their lunch. Over lunch, describe in detail the routines you have previously identified and what you dislike about them. Then ask this person what new courses of action he or she might suggest to breathe new life and activity into old, tired routines. Sometimes a fresh set of eyes can see clearly the possibilities to which we have become blind.

3. Spend one day a month working at a job other than your own.

Volunteer to do the job of a subordinate, a peer, and when appropriate, even a superior. Explain that your request is based on your desire to better understand the overall working of your organization, to learn more broad-based skills and to develop stronger, more collaborative working relationships. In the process, this change of pace, change of scenery and activity, allows you to step out of your routines temporarily, thereby infusing you with new insights and energy regarding how you might better serve your clients.

Secret # 3

Give Customers Your Undivided Attention

*That thing is for gettin' customers.
It's not for worryin' 'em once I get' em.
You don't mind, do ya, Phil?*
– Willie Watson

Millions of people hit the floor *running* each day. We *run* from home to work. At work, we *run* from one meeting to the next. Between meetings, during snippets of conversations, we complain that deadlines and our calendars are *running* our lives. Midday, we grab a bite to eat on the *run* as we head out to *run* errands. When the workday is finally through, the race we are *running* is far from over. We leave work and *run* by our child's soccer practice on our way to the gym. At the gym, we jump on the treadmill (ironic isn't it?) and *run* a couple of miles in an effort to maintain a level of health and fitness that will enable us to keep *running* No one can question our commitment to the activity of our life. But, we question the value of what we have accomplished through that activity.

As service providers, we find ourselves in a very similar situation. We run from season to season, promotion to promotion, customer to customer in hopes of landing the next major contract or the next big sale that will guarantee our business success. Our effort is an honest one. We're doing our best. Yet, our frustration grows as we come face-to-face with our lack of success and as we witness the lack of loyalty shown by those we are striving to serve.

Over the years, we have heard that all "good business" is founded on "good business relationships." It sounds fine. But what does it really mean?

And who has time to develop such relationships?

First, nobody has the time. There are always more pressing concerns to attend to. Yet, the most successful service professionals—pros like Willie—somehow make the time to develop positive, professional relationships with their customers, even when time available to do so is limited. They determine exactly what they can do to make their customers feel special. Often, it's as simple as seeing to it that the customer is given some undivided, much appreciated attention.

When I climbed into the front seat of that cab with Willie, I was on the run. I was running from the airport to the hotel and ultimately to my next engagement. Come to think of it, Willie was running, too. He was running this passenger to his destination before he ran back to the airport in search of additional fares before his shift was through.

This situation was ready-made for service mediocrity—or what I call a service "quick hitter." A "quick hitter" is a service situation in which the service provider does just enough to get by, but not enough to stand out or to really make a noticeable or lasting difference. If confronted concerning this "just enough" performance, the service provider would probably argue that she is doing exactly what she was supposed to do, exactly what she had been trained to do. She would probably be right. But we have now reached a point where "just enough" is "not good enough." As service professionals, it's only when we exceed the expectations of the customer that we become memorable. And when we become memorable, customers seem to want to repeat the experience and are willing to encourage others to experience the service for themselves.

Willie could have easily gotten me to my destination without much extra effort and he would have made a little money in the process. But had he not taken the time to show me special, undivided attention, it would have been an encounter that would have been quickly and easily forgotten. Instead, because of his efforts, Willie created a hard-to-forget situation steeped in service excellence.

Give Customers Your Undivided Attention

How did he do it? How did Willie develop that initial, unforgettable business relationship? Simply put, Willie intentionally put the spotlight on me.

Immediately after introducing himself and turning off his radio connection to his dispatcher, Willie offered me the following explanation, "That thing is for gettin' customers. It's not for worrin' 'em once I get 'em. You don't mind, do ya, Phil?"

With that one simple act and by way of the words that supported it, Willie both literally and symbolically gave indication that as of that moment, I had become the most important person in his world. As a customer, it was a unique feeling—a special feeling. One that I had not often experienced, but one that I instantly knew I wanted more of.

But let's face it. Willie is not the only service professional who has learned the importance and value of heaping attention on customers. Organizations can do it too, if they will. What's intriguing is there are so many different, yet wonderful, ways of giving the customer undivided attention and making him feel special in the process.

"Hey! Welcome to Cici's!"

When our children were young and we were still able to corral them in one place at the same time, our family enjoyed going out for pizza together. And when given the option as to where we would go for pizza, more often than not the kids would opt for Cici's. More literally, they would squeal for Cici's.

Cici's is a pizza restaurant chain that operated a store in our area. Located in the heart of a strip mall, the restaurant was known for offering a reasonably priced buffet with a wide variety of pizza choices. I can never remember visiting the restaurant when it was not crowded, often to overflowing. It was, without question, a popular restaurant. But there were lots of popular restaurants and lots of choices for pizza. What made our kids clamor to go to Cici's?

Willie's Way

Quite simply, Cici's staff made all the difference. Over time, our kids had grown to enjoy the lively greeting they were sure to receive upon entering the store. Regardless of how crowded the store was, every customer walking through the doors would be greeted with a loud, exuberant "HEY! WELCOME TO CICI'S" shout initiated by the person working the cash register, then echoed by other pizza makers and servers throughout the store. The staff seemed to genuinely enjoy the routine and so did my family.

The other thing that made Cici's special for us was despite the fact it was a pizza buffet the staff went out of their way to create made-to-order specialty pizzas for their patrons. The pizza "chefs" would look up from behind their mounds of pizza dough and address customers making their way to the buffet counter. These pizza makers, sometimes two or three at a time, would shout from their positions behind the counter and ask patrons, "What kind of pizza do you like?"

If the buffet offered an ample supply of what the guest was looking for, the answer might be, "It's all right here. I'm fine, thanks." However, if a preferred pizza option was not currently available on the buffet line, "Pepperoni, sausage, and green peppers, please," might be the patron's reply.

"Coming your way in six minutes," would be the enthusiastic comeback. "Thanks for eating at Cici's."

Six minutes later, a fresh, hot pepperoni, sausage, and green pepper pizza made especially for the guest would be delivered directly to his table. It was a small thing that literally any pizza restaurant could do for its clientele. However, Cici's not only did it, but they made a bit of a production out of doing it, thereby inserting both fun and festivity into the equation. For a few seconds, the staff gave all patrons their undivided attention. And it made a difference. I know.

After each visit, on the drive home, our kids would be shouting, "HEY! WELCOME TO CICI'S ... HEY! WELCOME TO CICI'S ... HEY! WELCOME TO CICI'S ..." to no one in particular. They had simply caught the enthusiasm of those who had just served them.

Give Customers Your Undivided Attention

When was the last time you or your family left an eating establishment literally shouting with glee? Cici's food—and the overall service experience—left a good taste in our mouths. We returned to revisit the experience often.

I don't know whether or not Willie Watson has ever eaten at a Cici's pizza restaurant, but somehow I suspect he would appreciate their unique approach to paying attention to the customer. Acknowledging customers immediately, changing a routine activity into anything but routine, and making the customer feel special in the process were all classic examples of offering service "Willie's Way."

But it's not just a restaurant or company that can create that attitude of focused attention on the customer. Individuals can—and should—as well.

We Escort Our Guests

When it comes to hotels, I must admit that I am fairly jaded. I am not proud of the fact, but it is a fact nevertheless. I have become a bit cynical for two basic reasons. First, for the past 17 years or so, my job has required that I spend up to 150 days a year on the road. Or said a different way, that's 150 nights a year that I've spent sleeping in a bed other than my own. It's safe to assume that the excitement of going to a "nice hotel" has long since worn off for me.

Second, because I speak at a great number of large conferences and conventions around the world, I have had the opportunity to stay at some of the finest hotels in existence. I continue to be amazed at their size, splendor, and overall magnificence, but when it comes time to retire for the evening, my wants and needs are fairly basic. I want a warm, safe, quiet, comfortable environment with no surprises. That's pretty much it. If a hotel intends to impress me with its service, it will have to do more than hang terry cloth robes in the closet or pile mounds of throw pillows on the bed.

As jaded as I was, I must admit that my expectations for the Ritz Carlton were pretty high. I expected the facility to be beautiful. I also had been looking forward to observing the hotel's staff firsthand. The Ritz Carlton was well-known for its motto: "We are ladies and gentlemen serving ladies and gentlemen." I wanted to see if they would live up to their own hype.

I arrived at the Ritz Carlton on Florida's Amelia Island shortly before midnight. I had just driven in from the Jacksonville Airport. It had been a long day and I knew it was going to be a short night. The clock told me I only had a few hours to rest before I was to speak the next morning to a group of aviation executives.

As I crossed the lobby heading toward the registration desk, I barely noticed how beautiful the lobby was. The staff members I encountered were professional and courteous, but I hardly noticed them either. All I really wanted to do at that point was to find the way to my room and to fall in bed. The desk clerk accommodated me and I was soon down for the night.

I slept fast. By 6:15 a.m., I was out the door and headed for the convention center to check out the meeting room I would be speaking in later that morning. This early morning room check was one of my professional rituals. I knew if I found anything to be out of order there was still plenty of time for corrections and changes to be made before the participants began arriving. I had learned over time that coming early and taking care of the lingering details served to lessen my anxiety level and provide a better overall experience for my customers.

I blazed a circuitous trail from my room through the empty hallways of the hotel in search of the convention center. Once the convention center had been discovered, I continued to seek out the room in which I was scheduled to speak. Finally, I located the meeting room. Upon entering the room I was pleased, but not surprised to find the room set exactly as I had requested.

There is no need for any changes to be made this time. The room looks great. I've still got time to go have a leisurely breakfast and read the paper.

Give Customers Your Undivided Attention

I stepped out of the meeting room and back into the spacious lobby of the Ritz Carlton convention center. I suddenly realized that I was completely turned around. My sense of direction had failed me.

My gosh, I'm lost. I have no idea how to get to the restaurant from here.

About that time, two female members of the housekeeping staff rounded the corner, headed in my general direction. While still quite a distance off, one went out of her way to speak to me.

"Good morning, sir. Is there something I can help you with this morning?"

"I'm a little confused," I admitted. "Would you please point me toward the restaurant?"

At the sound of my words, the lady who spoke first changed her direction and headed directly toward me. Without any other words being spoken, the other woman peeled off and went about her business.

"Sir, please follow me," she said politely.

For the next couple of minutes, I followed dutifully as this middle-aged lady led me up one hallway and down another. We talked casually as we walked and I learned her name was Maria. Finally, the restaurant came into sight at the end of the hall. As we approached, Maria spoke to the restaurant's hostess.

"Linda, this gentleman is interested in joining you for breakfast."

Linda took the cue and acted accordingly. "Welcome, sir, we're glad to have you. If you will please follow me, I will be happy to seat you now. Would you prefer smoking or nonsmoking this morning?"

"Nonsmoking," I said as I fell in lockstep behind Linda. Just then, I realized Maria was no longer beside me. Their pass-off had been so seamless I hardly knew it had happened. I stopped in my tracks.

"Linda, excuse me, for just a moment," I said, as I turned to see Maria retreating. "Maria, one minute please."

59

Hearing my words, Maria stopped and turned to face me.

"Yes, sir? Is there something else I can help you with?" she asked.

"No, there's nothing else. I just wanted to thank you for your help. It was very kind of you, but you really didn't have to bring me all the way here. You could have just pointed the way and I'm sure I would have found it eventually."

Maria looked me in the eye as she squared her body to mine. Then she smiled and responded with a combination of pride and confidence. I have never forgotten her words.

"Sir, at the Ritz Carlton we don't point our guests, we escort them."

It was at that moment I realized why the Ritz Carlton hotel chain had such a sterling reputation throughout the hospitality industry and with business and recreational travelers everywhere. It wasn't because of some unique configuration of brick and mortar. It wasn't because of a collection of first edition art on display. It was because of Maria, Linda, and hundreds of other staff members just like them who were committed to making even the briefest customer encounter memorable because of the personal, undivided attention they assigned to it.

I don't imagine that Maria, the housekeeper had ever ridden in Willie's cab. And I would be willing to bet money that Willie, the cab driver had never stayed in one of the Ritz Carlton rooms that Maria tended. Nevertheless, Willie and Maria were cut from the same bolt of cloth. They shared an innate commitment to treat their customers special—like ladies and gentlemen. After all, what else would you expect from such a lady and gentleman?

A Sign of the Times

But when things go sour in a relationship between a customer and a service provider, too often people end up acting like anything but ladies and gentle-

Give Customers Your Undivided Attention

men. That, too, draws attention—though not necessarily the attention we long for.

For several years, I drove the same 47 mile route two or three times a week, between the Gainesville, Florida, airport and my home in Ocala, Florida. I drove the route so frequently that I knew virtually every part of the highway intimately.

One morning on my trip north to Gainesville, something unusual caught my eye up ahead on the left. I could see that someone had propped a piece of plywood up against a tree, with the face of the board pointed toward the highway. I slowed down to get a better look. As I drew nearer, I saw something had been written on the wood in red paint. I pulled off the road and read the following hand-lettered message:

I MADE A $13,000 MISTAKE BY BUYING A MOBILE HOME FROM [COMPANY NAME WITHHELD]

Though I had absolutely no details regarding the impetus behind the sign, the sign itself and the message it conveyed intrigued me. As I resumed my drive to the Gainesville airport, my mind began to wander.

I wonder what that sign was all about? I wonder how long it has been up? I wonder if it was written by a male or a female? I wonder how old the person was that wrote it? I wonder if the mobile home company knows it is there? I wonder what will happen next as a result of the sign? I wonder how many people have seen that sign?

My brief exposure to the sign created far more questions than answers. But the single question I kept coming back to time after time involved how many people might have seen the sign.

The road is well traveled. Many people pass this way. It has to be a big number.

By the time I got to the airport, my curiosity had gotten the better of me. I decided to do some research. One simple phone call to the Florida

Department of Transportation yielded all the information I needed. I was told that more than 5,000 cars a day traveled that particular route between Ocala and Gainesville.

But common sense told me all those cars weren't single-passenger vehicles. So, as an arithmetic exercise, I decided to estimate that on average each car carried two people. Simple math then told me that at least 10,000 people each day traveling Highway 441 north and south had the same exposure and the same opportunity to read the same sign I had read. Therefore, I felt it safe to assume that at least 10,000 people each day could have their attention drawn negatively to this particular business based on the message the sign conveyed.

When I returned from my trip two days later, I noticed the sign again. I multiplied 10,000 per day times two. Now we were up to 20,000 negative exposures in just two days.

In the days that followed, as I made trip after trip to and from Gainesville, I began to look for the sign. In fact, it became a landmark for me (and I wondered how many others). It never left—for six weeks! With each new sighting, I would add to my previous totals. The number grew steadily, until after six weeks, my simple calculations told me we were fast approaching a half million negative exposures!

Then the inevitable day finally came. I was headed to Gainesville for yet another trip when I noticed the sign was gone.

Well, he must finally be over being upset, I chuckled to myself, even though I had no specific knowledge the sign-maker was a "he." *I wonder if he worked things out with the business or if he just finally decided to give up? If he did work it out with the business, I wonder if it was some sort of "gentlemen's agreement" or if lawyers got involved? I wonder what the long-term effect of this whole thing will be on both parties? Whatever the case, the whole thing has made driving back and forth more interesting for me.*

Give Customers Your Undivided Attention

As far as I was concerned, the issue was over. That is until I made my return trip from the airport a few days later. Out of habit, I looked for the old sign. It was still gone. But what I saw in its place was even more amazing.

Where the old hand-lettered plywood sign had once rested against the tree, there was now a new professionally painted sign displaying the same message. This one meticulously stenciled and featuring vibrant, eye-catching colors. This one mounted higher up on the tree, thereby providing better visual impact for both north and southbound lanes of traffic. This one had taken more thought, effort, and money.

Amazing! I can hardly believe the lengths that people will go to get attention, I thought.

That's just the point. On the one hand, if customers are disrespected enough, disgusted enough, desperate enough, and determined enough, they will go to great lengths to have others pay attention to their service plight.

On the other hand, when service professionals masterfully turn the spotlight on the customer, good things happen.

It's Simple—Service Sells

It was the fourth or fifth time in the past several months that I had wandered through the Johnston & Murphy shoe store located in the Atlanta airport. I had been on the lookout for a new pair of black dress shoes and I trusted the Johnston & Murphy brand. From previous experience, I knew the company produced a shoe that would look good and wear well over time. The company's reputation for producing quality products was sterling. And like many others, I was willing to pay for quality.

Then why hadn't I bought the shoes during one of the previous visits? Frankly, it was the service. During each of my earlier visits, I had been basically ignored. After the obligatory, "Can I help you?" from the sales clerk on duty, it seemed I was soon relegated to the perceived ranks of "browser" not "buyer."

Willie's Way

Maybe it was the jeans I prefer to wear when traveling. I might not have looked like the typical Johnston & Murphy customer. Maybe it was something about my demeanor. Or maybe the clerks I had encountered simply had bigger fish to fry—more important things to do than wait on me. I really didn't know. All I knew for sure was that no clerk had ever given me more than 10 seconds of their time.

On the way to my gate, I had spotted the familiar Johnston & Murphy sign at the top of the escalator in Terminal B. My flight wasn't scheduled to leave for several more minutes, so I allowed myself the opportunity to pause once again and hover briefly over a slick pair of black lace-ups. Though I really wanted and needed the shoes, I wasn't seriously considering making the purchase. Maybe it had become one of those self-fulfilling prophesies—the clerks at Johnston & Murphy had previously seen me as nothing more than a "window shopper," and now I had become one. I was there for less than a minute when I heard someone speak.

"It looks like your carry-on is getting a little beat up."

I glanced up to see a stranger smiling at me. The young man's nametag read "Johnston & Murphy—Eric."

"As much as I travel, I've stopped trying to keep my travel bags looking like new," I admitted. "It's a losing battle."

"Well, I'm sure we can make it look better," he responded over his shoulder, while retreating to the sales counter. He returned quickly with a container in hand, knelt and began vigorously rubbing mink oil into my bag's gouged and scarred leather. As he worked, he began to share helpful tips intended to enhance the beauty and prolong the life of fine leather products.

He was knowledgeable, genuine, and enthusiastic. As he spoke and rubbed, the original shine and luster began to reappear in the worn leather. I was impressed by the effort and the outcome.

Give Customers Your Undivided Attention

"There, that's much better, don't you think?" he asked, as he stood once again. Not waiting for the obvious answer, he continued. "I noticed you admiring the black pair. Would you like to try them on?" I glanced at my watch. I still had time.

"Sure. I wear a size nine and a half, please."

Eric turned, left, and reappeared with a box under his arm. In seconds, he was once again on his knees, this time with a shoehorn in hand instead of the mink oil. With professional flair and confidence, Eric used the shoehorn to guide my right, then left foot into first one shoe and then the other. As he laced, he told me about the workmanship that goes into every pair of Johnston & Murphy shoes. He talked about how to extend the life of the shoes by way of proper care and storage. And, as importantly, he told me how good they looked on my feet—despite the jeans I was wearing. In the end, the decision was simply a no-brainer.

"I'll take them."

I actually enjoyed the walk with Eric toward the cash register. I was confident in my purchase, because I was confident that I had been led to that purchase by a competent and dedicated service professional. But Eric wasn't finished yet. En route, Eric called my attention to a belt that matched my shoes perfectly. I wasn't really in the market for a belt, but what the heck, I told him to ring it up, too.

As Eric wrapped each shoe individually before placing them in their box, I asked, "Eric, I've never seen you before. How long have you been working here?"

"Only two weeks," he said. "But, I'm sure I'm going to like it here. I enjoy helping people."

I just smiled and nodded my head.

I hope these folks appreciate this guy. He's as good as money in the bank. Look what he did with me. He paid a little attention to me and my needs and the next thing I know I'm handing him my credit card.

The final tally came to $202.66. As he took my credit card, Eric looked up smiling and said, "Oh, I almost forgot. Would you like a bottle of the mink oil to take with you for your bag. It's only $5.99."

"No thanks," I said, laughing. "I think I've been softened up enough already."

Putting It Into Practice

Giving customers your undivided attention is not always easy, but it is always necessary. Willie Watson did it by turning off his radio. Maria did it by going out of her way to escort a guest to breakfast. Eric did it by dropping to his knees to apply a little mink oil and elbow grease. But, regardless of how the "gift of attention" is packaged, wrapped, and delivered, the customer will always appreciate receiving it.

Here are three ideas (out of dozens of possibilities) that might help you get started focusing your attention more clearly on the customer:

1. Get to know your customers.

Undivided attention doesn't get any better than being able to recognize your customers by sight and identify them by name. Service professionals do whatever is necessary to become more proficient at remembering names. Read books or take classes on memory enhancement, recognition through association or any other method that will show your customers that you have focused a considerable amount of attention specifically on them. Create index card-type "cheat sheets" for each of your valuable customers on which you list pertinent information and facts. Review and refer to the cards often. Continuously add additional customer information to the cards as it becomes available to you.

2. Set the tone early.

When it is time to interact with the customer directly, make sure they know they are at the very center of your attention. Let them know how much time you have available for them. Invite them to join you in your office, a conference room, or for a walk to ensure the two of you will not be disturbed. If you invite them into your office, make a point of asking your secretary or a coworker—in the presence of the customer—to please field your calls while you are with the customer.

3. Ask, shut up, and listen.

Don't be afraid to ask questions, even probing questions. The more focused and tailored the questions, the more apparent it will be to customers that your attention is fixed on them. However, it is very important that once you ask the questions—you must stop talking. A common tendency for even the most dedicated service professional is to talk (for the purpose of telling all he knows and how he knows) when he should be listening. Remember, silence can be your friend. More often that not, your customer will rush to fill whatever silence exists with information that may prove to be valuable to you in the future. Let the customer talk as much as possible—you listen.

Secret # 4

Listen, Think, and Use Common Sense

How do ya plan to get back to the airport?
– Willie Watson

Have you ever met an "average person?"

I read books and articles regularly that seem to take great pleasure in referencing and describing in detail the "average man," the "average woman," the "average baby," the "average teenager," the "average American," the "average college graduate," the "average high school dropout," the "average retiree," the "average working mother." The list goes on and on. Whenever I see such descriptions, I immediately get suspicious. Why? Because so far, I have never met an average person.

I admit that I have met individuals who exhibit some of the characteristics attributed to "average-ness." For example, I recently read that the "average American male is five feet, nine inches tall." That got my attention. I'm an American male and I am five feet, nine inches tall.

Maybe I've finally found the average person I've been searching for after all. And it's me!

However, in the next paragraph I went on to read that this five foot, nine inch American male "on average weighs 165 pounds."

Oops. All of a sudden, I'm not average any more.

Think about it. The notion of "average" is simply a manufactured concept. In its truest sense, it is a mathematical attempt to group and measure *things* logically. But we must always remember that people are not things. Therefore, the "average label" seldom, if ever, should be applied to people. Attempting to force individuals into predetermined categories designed to group, measure, and explain average intellect, average attitude, or average performance may, in reality, serve to rob these same individuals of their native creativity, imagination, motivation, and ultimately their individual uniqueness. It boils down to this. If we tell individuals they are average often enough—or treat them as if there is nothing special about them—too many of them will eventually begin to believe it and will begin to consciously strive to be average.

And another thing. Who really wants to be average anyway? Not me. I recognize that we can't be great at *everything,* but there's absolutely no reason to believe each of us can't be great at *something.* We should never be satisfied when we find ourselves or our departments being described as average. We should go all out to be excellent in something. As service professionals our constant, unfailing purpose should be to relentlessly strive to develop a level of recognizable service excellence in all that we do for our customers, be they internal or external.

I suppose it could be argued by some narrow-minded researcher that Willie Watson was an average, middle-aged man, living in an average city, driving an average looking cab, working for an average laborer's wage, while serving the needs of average travelers. Under such circumstances, it would be reasonable to believe that Willie's passengers should expect nothing more than average service from this average guy. Right?

Wrong! Why? Because looks can be deceiving and impressions may be misleading. Willie Watson was anything but average. Willie distinguished himself in a number of ways. As a result, Willie had developed himself into an "above average" service professional.

While Willie may have lacked the ability to articulate profound service ideals, he excelled in his ability to listen with focus and clarity of mind. While Willie may have lacked the ability to philosophize and pontificate,

Listen, Think, and Use Common Sense

he impressed with his ability to think and reason effectively. And while Willie may have been lacking in formal advanced education, he more than compensated with his application of common sense.

As I recall our initial encounter, I now realize Willie may have been at his very best when he was listening to me. But it wasn't a general, manufactured "Oh, really?" "I didn't know that," "How interesting!" type listening. No, Willie's listening was focused and purposeful. He needed specific information so that he could serve me better. Therefore, he took no chances. He asked questions that required specific answers. Questions like, "Phil, what brings ya to Columbia, anyhow?" "Phil, when ya leavin' town?" "Will ya be headed home?" "Well, how do ya plan to get back to the airport?"

As he asked each question and then sat back and listened to my answers, he was mentally formulating a tailor-made plan of service he would soon offer me, his customer. Willie's technique need not be unique to this South Carolina cab driver. Others can and should be using the technique for their own customer service purposes.

I Prefer Peach Yogurt

Several years ago, I hosted a Business Leadership Academy that drew leaders from all over the United States. For three days, the entire staff of my company —Susan, my wife, Kim, our Office Manager, and I attended to the physical, emotional, and intellectual needs of this very elite group of leaders.

It was an exciting time. I had partnered with some of the finest leadership experts in the country. The educational sessions we presented were thought-provoking and interactive. The spirited discussions that resulted proved to be challenging and intellectually stimulating. Our intent was not only to preach the value of leadership enhancement and service excellence to the assembled group. We also tried to model it in all we did for the group.

Besides the education element, we spared no expense and took no shortcuts with lodging, entertainment, and of course, food. The old saying, "The way to a man's heart is through his stomach," works for me. Therefore, I've also reasoned that the way to an audience member's mind is through his or her stomach. I figured, feed them well and they will think better. So we did.

Each morning started with a full breakfast buffet. Bacon, sausage, eggs, pastries, fruit, cereal, and all the fixings. The noontime and evening meals were just as elaborate. It was our unwritten goal that participants would leave the gathering with both their intellectual and physical needs satisfied.

On the first morning of the academy, all was ready. The hotel banquet staff had done a wonderful job in preparation and presentation of breakfast. At the appropriate times, the doors swung open and in streamed our hungry attendees. They descended on the buffet line with great enthusiasm. Susan, Kim, and I spread out around the room, working each table and greeting each participant individually. If there were to be any problems, we were intent on identifying, isolating, and correcting them early on. Thankfully, there seemed to be none.

As I moved to one of the tables, I was greeted warmly by eight registrants enjoying their breakfasts. While chatting briefly with the group, I noticed one of the eight simply having coffee. The sight struck me as odd by comparison—everyone else eating except this one.

I now realize I *should* have trusted my instincts. I *should* have asked the question that was on my mind, *"Why aren't you eating?"* I *should* have listened carefully to his response. But honestly, I didn't do any of those things. That was my mistake. Instead, I simply dismissed the thought and moved on to the next table. Frankly, I was more interested in glad-handing and wallowing in the praise I was receiving than to worry about minor, unsubstantiated concerns. Little did I realize I had just walked past a prime service opportunity—an opportunity to demonstrate my service professionalism.

Thankfully, our office manager, Kim soon approached the same table. Like me, she noticed the individual nursing his coffee while the others around

Listen, Think, and Use Common Sense

him ate heartily. But, unlike me, Kim took the initiative to ask the appropriate question and to listen carefully to the answer it elicited.

"Mr. Roberts, is there anything I can get for you?" she asked, as she knelt beside the coffee drinker's chair.

"No, thanks. I'm fine," was the soft-spoken reply.

"But, you're not eating. It's going to be a long day," Kim protested mildly. "I would be happy to get you something. Is there anything specifically you would like?"

The gentleman smiled meekly and confided to Kim, "I hate to admit it, but I am a very picky eater and a creature of habit. Everything looks delicious, but I have eaten the same breakfast every day for years. I always have coffee and yogurt. But not just any yogurt. It's a little embarrassing, but I prefer peach yogurt. I checked with the banquet staff and they don't have any here. But, that's okay, I'm sure I can live without it for a couple of days."

He didn't have to. Later that day, Kim made an unscheduled trip to the grocery store and purchased enough peach yogurt for the gentleman to enjoy during the balance of the conference. The next morning, you can imagine the gentleman's surprise when Kim presented him with his own personal supply of peach yogurt and assured him there was more available where that came from.

It's important to note that Kim neither asked my permission nor waited for my directive on this seemingly insignificant matter. She didn't need to. She had asked the question of the customer and she had heard the response. She knew there was something she could do to make this gentleman's conference experience more pleasurable. She simply did it with no fanfare. In fact, I didn't even learn of Kim's personalized service feat until after the conference had concluded.

As I sat in the privacy of my office reading the academy's participant evaluations, I marveled at what Mr. Roberts had written. He had given the conference the highest marks possible in every category. But he saved his highest written praise for Kim and her focus on his individual needs. He stressed that her actions were the most practical demonstration of personal leadership and customized service that he had ever witnessed. He finished his written evaluation by stating his intention to send an even larger delegation of his subordinates to our future leadership conferences.

Mr. Roberts didn't write specifically about the quality of the instruction at the conference or the new leadership perspectives he acquired. Instead, he wrote about how Kim had listened to his needs and responded accordingly. It was service in action. Though neither she nor Mr. Roberts would have explained it as such, Kim was doing it "Willie's Way."

But there are still other classic examples of service professionals who listen and respond to their customers in meaningful ways.

Service Is Spelled S-A-Z-E-R-A-C

The conversation was pleasant. Earlier in the day I had presented a service professionalism training program for the Georgia Club Managers' Association, a group of managers representing some of the finest city, athletic, golf, and country clubs throughout the state of Georgia. Now I found myself dining with nine of the most highly respected leaders in the field of club management. Somewhere between the appetizer and the salad, Manuel de Juan, general manager of the host Capital City Club spoke.

"Phillip, I thoroughly enjoyed your presentation today. I especially enjoyed the stories you shared to illustrate your content points. I found the experience to be very appropriate and beneficial for what we do," he said, with an easy lilt in his voice that made his accent even more engaging. "As a matter of fact, at one point during your presentation, I almost interrupted you to share one of my stories I thought you might enjoy."

Curious, I said, "Manuel, I wish you had interrupted me. But since you didn't, would you be willing to share your story with all of us now?"

Listen, Think, and Use Common Sense

Manuel proceeded to share one of the most encouraging examples of service professionalism I have ever heard. I'm certain Willie Watson himself would have been proud.

The occasion was Easter Sunday and the day found more than 500 club members and their guests crowded into the overflowing Capital City Club restaurant. As they waited to dine, a club member and his four dinner guests approached the bar where they were greeted by the head bartender, Bob. Bob quickly and professionally began to take and fill each drink order. Everything progressed as might be expected until one of the guests placed an order for a specialty drink.

"I would like a *sazerac,* please."

"A sazerac?" Bob asked curiously. "Sir, I'm sorry but I'm unfamiliar with that particular drink. However, if you'll share its ingredients with me, I will be happy to make you one."

"That's the problem," the guest explained. "I was in New Orleans on business recently and I stayed at the Fairmont Hotel. During my visit, I went into the hotel bar and the bartender suggested I try the house specialty, a *sazerac*. I remember the name of the drink because it was the same as that of the bar. Anyway, I tried the drink and I loved it. Since then though, whenever I've tried to order it in other bars around the country I always get the same response, 'never heard of it.' I was hoping a place like the Capital City Club would be different. But never mind. Don't worry about it. Just give me a Bloody Mary instead."

Bob worked quickly to fill the revised drink order. As soon as the guest left the bar with drink in hand to rejoin his party, Bob took his break and headed straight to the nearest telephone. He called information and requested the number for the Fairmont Hotel in New Orleans, Louisiana. Once connected to the Fairmont, Bob asked for the Sazerac Bar. Within seconds, Bob was talking directly with a previously anonymous professional colleague in a bar several hundred miles away.

Willie's Way

"My name is Bob and I am the head bartender at the Capital City Club here in Atlanta. A few minutes ago I had a gentleman order a *sazerac*. He told me he was introduced to it while visiting your bar. I was wondering if you would be willing to share the recipe with me so I can fill his order?"

Bob's New Orleans counterpart was happy to oblige.

Within a few short minutes, Bob confidently approached the guest's table. Imagine the guest's level of surprise, satisfaction, and sheer delight when Bob said, "Excuse me, sir, but I have your *sazerac*. I hope it's to your liking. I have taken the liberty of writing down the ingredients on this index card so you can have them with you in your travels. I hope you enjoy your time here at the Capital City Club. I'm glad I had the opportunity to serve you."

What makes this story and Bob, the bartender, so extraordinary? The most important thing—Bob listened carefully and responded to what he heard. It somehow feels as if it should be more complicated than that. But it's not! Like Willie, Bob's actions provide a glimpse of the service possibilities and what can be accomplished when listening, imagination, and initiative are intertwined.

But listening is only one part of what sets true service professionals apart from service imposters. Willie was a good listener, but he was also a clear, concise thinker.

Once Willie had listened—and learned—that I was in town on business, that I had a tight travel schedule and that I couldn't afford to miss my plane the next day, it was then a simple process of thinking about the possibilities and deciding what course of action would be most appropriate.

Remember what he told me? "First thing ya need to know is that gettin' a cab on a Sunday 'round here could be a challenge."

With that simple statement, I began to realize Willie was thinking about me, not himself. He was thinking about my unique situation and beginning to help me determine my options. All customers appreciate knowing that the service provider is thinking about the customer's best interests, not their own.

Listen, Think, and Use Common Sense

But is this a sound business philosophy? Of course it is. Organizations that are in business to sell their products and services don't bet their future on one-time sales. On the contrary. They strive to build a strong business foundation based on repeat business. They have come to realize that should an established customer choose never to do business with the company again, that single decision could amount to hundreds, thousands, or even hundreds of thousands of lost dollars and opportunities in the months, years and decades ahead.

So it is important to listen carefully to our customers. In listening to our customers, we learn what they want, need, and expect from us. At that point, as service professionals, it becomes our responsibility to create a thoughtful, strategically sound approach for providing efficient, effective, and profitable service. Whether the organization consists of one person or thousands, our long-term success depends on how well we listen, think, and act.

When Is a Greeter Not Just a Greeter?

It was the summer of 1979. I was one semester short of graduating from Murray State University with a degree in Marketing Management. That summer I applied for and was hired as a summer employee at the local Wal-Mart Store in Princeton, Kentucky. It was my first non-agricultural job. For the next three months, I worked selling oil filters and fishing lures to automotive and sporting goods bargain shoppers. It was an interesting and enjoyable change of pace from the farm.

A few weeks before I was scheduled to leave my job at Wal-Mart and return to school, I was approached by one of Wal-Mart's assistant managers, a young man named Gregg.

"Phil, we've been watching you this summer and we've been impressed with the attitude and effort you've displayed since you've been here," he told me. "Our company is growing and we believe there is a future at Wal-Mart for industrious individuals such as you. Therefore, on behalf of the company

Willie's Way

I would like to offer you an opportunity to join our management trainee program here at Wal-Mart. If you are interested, we will hold a position open for you until you graduate at the end of the semester. What do you think, Phil? Would you like to be a full-time member of the Wal-Mart management team?"

I remember being surprised and flattered by the offer. I also remember exactly what I told Gregg that day. My simple, but honest response revealed a less than brilliant, futuristic business mind. It's laughable today, but it's also true. I looked at Gregg and said, "No thanks, Gregg. When I get out of college I want to work for a big company."

Today Wal-Mart is the single largest retailer in the world. Its existence arguably represents one of the greatest business success stories of the twentieth and now twenty-first centuries. Wal-Mart has thousands of stores worldwide, well over a million and a half employees and annual sales that are about one quarter of a *trillion* dollars. Its scope of influence and impact is virtually unprecedented.

Though I could never have predicted the phenomenal success Wal-Mart would realize in the years following that conversation, I remember something special about the company even way back then. Under Mr. Sam's (as Wal-Mart founder, Sam Walton was affectionately known) leadership, Wal-Mart was absolutely committed to satisfying their local customers. I saw firsthand Wal-Mart's unprecedented inclination to give customers refunds for products that were returned without a sales receipt, for products obviously damaged during use, and even for products that had been purchased at one of Wal-Mart's competitors.

Way back then I questioned the wisdom of such a liberal return policy.

How can any company afford to give refunds so easily? Don't they realize that people will take advantage of them? Don't they realize that normal businesses just don't do things like that?

Listen, Think, and Use Common Sense

Exactly! Wal-Mart was never interested in being compared to other companies. They always saw themselves as being different. The refund policy, for example, was explained to me very simply. "Phil, Wal-Mart has chosen to do business in small southern towns where most of the local people either know one another or are related to one another. Therefore, we realize if we tick off one customer, it's possible that one customer will have influence with dozens more." Alienating even small numbers of customers was a risk the early leaders of Wal-Mart seemed unwilling to take. The trusting return policy continued.

But not everyone is to be trusted. A very small percentage of customers began taking further advantage of the policy by taking product off the store's shelves or racks, ripping away the price tags, and then carrying the products to the front of the store for a cash refund. They were stealing from the company without even removing the products from the premises. And Wal-Mart management knew it was happening.

But to their credit they didn't overreact. They didn't rush out and hire off-duty, uniformed police officers and security guards as is the practice of some major department stores. That tactic was not in keeping with the small-town feeling Wal-Mart had worked to develop and wished to retain. Instead, they took time to carefully think about the situation before taking action. The result of this focused thinking was "greeters."

Enter any Wal-Mart store, any place in the world today and you will come face-to-face with a greeter. These folks are usually friendly senior citizens who are quick to offer a shopping cart, a smile, and even a pleasant greeting. But contrary to what their title might suggest, the primary purpose of a store greeter is not the act of greeting, but rather store security.

Greeters visually survey each entering shopper to determine if they are bringing anything with them into the store. If so, they ask the customer if the item is to be returned. A color-coded sticker is applied to the customer's package and the greeter then directs the shopper to the return desk adjacent to the store's entrance. The process is so discreet and nonthreatening that honest customers don't feel threatened by it, while dishonest customers feel compelled to do their stealing elsewhere.

If the largest retailer in the world can think and employ simple strategies that will not compromise their relationship with their customers, surely the rest of us can as well.

The total package then is to listen, think, and use common sense in the way we treat our customers. It sounds too easy—too good to be true. Unfortunately, for many people and organizations, it is too good to be true. Some service providers don't want to listen to the customer; they have been conditioned to react, not think; and possibly worst of all, for too many organizations, common sense is in short supply.

Service Is Common Sense

I fly a lot. Over 1,900 flight segments in the past 17 years alone. On average, I will take off and land with one air carrier or another about 125 times each year. But, for the better part of 15 years, there was one particular airline to whom I chose to give the majority of my air travel business. I have opted not to reveal the name of the airline here. Instead, I will simply refer to them as my *previously preferred carrier* or PPC. During that extended period, I was flying with my PPC between 75 and 100 times annually, resulting in several thousand dollars each year in fares. This PPC was never the most economical of choices, but I felt a certain amount of loyalty to them.

In the summer of 2001, a few months before the tragedy that has become known as 9/11, I had to fly from Orlando to Indianapolis for a business meeting. To accommodate my client's schedule, I planned to fly up one morning, meet and return the following morning. I made my travel arrangements accordingly, choosing to utilize the services of my PPC.

The day before the trip, my client called and informed me it would be necessary to abbreviate our meeting somewhat. He suggested we meet as

Listen, Think, and Use Common Sense

soon as I arrived, possibly allowing me the opportunity to fly back home that same evening. A frequent "road warrior" himself, he understood the value of one more night at home with family. It sounded good to me.

I arrived at the Orlando airport at approximately 5:00 a.m. for the first leg of my trip to Indianapolis. I was the only customer in line. The ticketing agent, G.A. (her initials), was pleasant and professional. I explained my desire to return to Orlando that evening, as opposed to the next morning, if possible. G.A. confirmed that there was a direct flight from Indianapolis to Orlando leaving at 6:50 p.m. and according to the "load report" several seats were still available. "It shouldn't be a problem at all to stand by for that flight," she assured me. I thanked her and immediately called and cancelled my hotel reservation in Indianapolis for that evening. Before long, I was on my way.

After a successful day of meetings, I arrived back at the Indianapolis airport just after 4:00 p.m. that same afternoon for the 6:50 p.m. flight back to Orlando. When I checked in, the Indianapolis ticket agent (name unknown) informed me that I could not fly standby since my ticket had me returning the next day. I explained that her Orlando counterpart had assured me earlier there would be no problem. Unmoved, she coldly explained there was a problem. I could either pay an additional $100 and fly today, otherwise, "No exceptions."

"Are there seats available on the flight?" I asked.

"Yes, there are seats available," she admitted, but she went on to inform me that this was a matter of strict "company policy."

Was it just "company policy" in Indianapolis? Because this morning the folks in Orlando were apparently working under a different policy.

I was irritated, but composed. I asked to speak to the agent's supervisor. The gate agent huffed noticeably as she walked to the supervisor standing a few feet away. The two huddled and whispered, occasionally stealing quick, glaring glances my way. Finally, both approached with the supervisor in the lead.

"Sir, the agent has explained your request to me," she stated coldly, not offering me the opportunity to speak, "and we will not be able to accommodate you as a standby passenger. It's against our policy."

I asked her name. "Penny," she responded flatly.

"Penny, as a supervisor, have you ever made an exception in a case like this?" The long, hard look she gave me was answer enough. Of course she had.

"Sir, I'm sorry, but this is our policy," she said, as she sidestepped my question. She didn't sound sorry at all.

"Penny, I would like you to go into your computer and look up my personal history with your airline and tell me what it says as of today." She was obviously not happy with my request, nevertheless she did as I asked.

"As of today, Mr. Van Hooser, you have 37,792 base miles for this year. You have 440,872 miles in your frequent flyer account and you have logged 1,905,872 total lifetime miles on our flights," she stated with cold efficiency.

"Okay, then let me get this straight. You are going to charge a long-standing customer—I believe your company refers to people like me as your 'elite million milers'—one who spends literally thousands of dollars each year with your company, an extra $100 to fly on a plane with, by your own admission, several empty seats, simply because I was originally scheduled to take the first flight out tomorrow morning instead of the last flight out tonight. Is that basically it?"

Without even a hint of pause to consider the possible repercussions of her answer and with no apparent concern for the idiocy of her response, Penny simply replied, "Yes, sir. That's our policy. Would you like a seat or not?"

My options were limited. I had already cancelled my hotel reservations and returned my rental car. She had me temporarily over a barrel. Whatever sense of loyalty I may have felt to this PPC before was quickly eroding. And it was obvious that Penny didn't seem to care.

Listen, Think, and Use Common Sense

As I handed the original agent my credit card, I was furious. But, I did not make a scene. Instead, with complete honesty and emotional control, I spoke directly to Penny and the agent.

"Please know that this whole thing makes absolutely no sense to me. But, I'm not going to make any foolish threats or promises I can't keep. For example, I'm not going to stand here and say I will never fly your airline again. The fact is I'm sure I will fly with you again. I have to. My travel options are limited and you both know it. But, whenever possible, I assure you I will give my business to airlines who work to please their customers, not to a company who is satisfied to let company policy override practical service and common sense."

Expressing my true feelings made me feel a little better. My emotions even subsided somewhat. That is until I boarded the flight and counted 74 (no exaggeration) empty seats. My ire rose again. Again, it just didn't make any sense!

I kept my word and immediately began to schedule flights on other carriers whenever possible. Several weeks later, I was scheduled to fly out of Tampa to my destination on one of my new choices, Southwest Airlines. Again, my meeting got rearranged at the last minute and the possibility presented itself that I might be able to return to Florida in time to attend one of my son's swim meets—an all too rare occurrence for me. However, to do so, my flight would have to be rescheduled. I would need to depart from and return to Orlando instead of Tampa as my initial travel itinerary had stated. Since I was holding confirmed, nonrefundable tickets (just like with my PPC) for the Tampa origination and return, and since the memory of my experience with my PPC was still fresh in my mind, I was concerned the additional change fees would be too high to make the change practical. Nevertheless, I figured it was worth a try. I called my travel agent and asked her to see what she could do. Later that day she called me back with the news.

"Phil, I just wanted you to know that the changes you requested have been made. You will be flying out of and back into Orlando on Southwest."

"How much extra is it going to cost me?" I asked, dreading the answer.

"Not an extra dime," she said proudly. "As a matter of fact, the ticket agent I spoke to asked that I relay a message to you personally. She asked me to tell you how happy they are that you chose to fly Southwest and they are pleased to be able to accommodate you at no extra charge. She said she wanted to be sure you know how much Southwest appreciates your business."

Since that day, I have continued to fly Southwest with greater regularity as I have continued to look for flight options other than those provided by my PPC. The practical net effect of the single experience described here, from a business perspective, is that I am now consciously diverting thousands of dollars each year from my PPC to Southwest and other carriers who seem genuinely interested in keeping my business.

Is there any wonder that Southwest Airlines has weathered the economic turmoil that has wreaked havoc on the airline industry in recent years, better than any other carrier in the United States? I'm not surprised. I'm convinced that common sense *is* good company policy!

Putting It Into Practice

Listening, thinking, and using common sense in service to customers is something that literally anyone interested in becoming a service professional can do. Whether it is supplying a customer with his favorite peach yogurt, supplying the guest a written recipe for his favorite drink, or redefining the job of store security, the process requires attention, imagination, and action.

Here are three ideas you may find helpful:

1. Ask better questions.

The best conversationalists are articulate, engaging, and generally fun to be around. They got that way, in part, by developing the fine art of asking good questions. Service pros are good at asking questions, too. They formulate and then ask questions designed to reveal what the customer is thinking, how the customer is feeling and what the customer wants to happen next (i.e., Ms. Jones, is the dinner party you are planning intended to celebrate some special occasion? Mr. Smith, since this will be your daughter's first car, what specific options do you want included or omitted? Mr. McDaniel, when would be the most convenient time for us to schedule your follow up appointment?) They ask questions in a conversational, not interrogational tone that makes responding to the questions more enjoyable.

2. Allow customers the time and opportunity to vent.

The activity of venting is the emotional equivalent of a relief valve letting steam out of a pressurized vessel. If there is no means of relief, the pressure will continue to build until the vessel can no longer withstand the strain it is under. Something will eventually give way. If we don't allow our customers the opportunity to vent to us periodically, they might just go to our competitors for the purpose of finding the relief they seek. As unpleasant as it is on occasion, this may prove to be a valuable investment of the service professional's time.

3. Remain poised and emotionally controlled.

Years ago, there was a deodorant commercial whose tag line was "never let 'em see you sweat." As a service professional, the same is true. When customers all around you are confused, irritated, or downright angry, the situation will never be improved by you losing your composure. Customers can and will say and do things that are inappropriate, uncalled for, and totally out of line. As service professionals, we don't have the same freedom. Grace, self-control, and professionalism under pressure are attributes used to describe the best of the best service pros. I hope these attributes describe you.

Secret # 5

Bend the Rules, Sometimes

*Now ya need to know something—
I don't do this for everybody.*
— Willie Watson

What are the most frustrating words a customer can hear? Go ahead, pick your favorite.

- "I won't be able to work you in for at least a couple of weeks."
- "Our computer is down, you will have to call back later."
- "We will send a service technician. You can expect him either today or tomorrow, sometime between 9:00 a.m. and 5:00 p.m."

Everyone, at one time or another, has had the experience of being a customer with a specific need, only to encounter unresponsive, unconcerned, lackadaisical service providers. As frustrating and infuriating as those experiences may have been, they can still serve as valuable learning opportunities. How? It's simple. Just pay close attention to what you thought and how you felt throughout those unpleasant service experiences. Then solemnly commit that you will never allow those same attitudes, actions, or habits to slip into your personal service efforts.

Yes, the statements listed are bad. But, in my opinion, they pale in comparison to the all-too-common, knee-jerk service retort I have grown to hate. Whenever I hear a service provider utter the following words, the hair on my neck stands on end, my teeth are set on edge, and I tense and brace for a fight. What provocative words could elicit such negative reactions?

"Policy says . . ."

In too many business environments today, organization representatives, both internal and external, have grown accustomed to using internal policies, rules, regulations, and the like as some sort of defensive weapon. A weapon designed primarily to keep their perceived enemy (a.k.a. the customer) at bay. That is wrong. Organizational policies should be established to build, not erode business relationships.

As customers get more interested in doing business with us, they naturally will be inclined to ask more probing questions while exploring various approaches to enhancing the business relationship. At such times, instead of fostering these positive attitudes and approaches, too many service providers almost instinctively throw up the "policy perimeter." The policy perimeter is established when we hear service providers saying things like, "I would love to help you, but our policy says . . ." or "I can't let you try that product out because our policy says . . ."

In essence, such statements (and the limited thought process behind them) communicate the following, "If we don't allow you, the customer, to breach our established policies, then we won't have to use imagination, creativity, and customized approaches to help you with your personal service issues. It will be easier for us if you do it our way." That's no way to woo, wow, and win customers and their loyalty.

Consider this question: Do restrictive policies help or hurt our overall service efforts? Here is the definitive answer—it just depends.

If specific policies have been established for maintaining a "high ground" position on moral, legal, and ethical issues facing our department or organization, then the policy is necessary—whether it helps or hurts service. But, if the policies have been established solely for our own convenience, with little thought or regard for the customer's needs and concerns, then that

Bend the Rules, Sometimes

policy will most certainly end up hurting our service efforts and ultimately, our business.

Here's why I'm adamant about the need to build flexibility into our established service policies. Let's assume all of the fifth graders and above in your local school system are asked to fill in the missing words for the following statement, *"Rules are made to _____."* What would be the answer most commonly offered?

Most would agree the vast majority of these young people would complete the phrase by saying, *"Rules are made to be broken."* Why? Even at a young, tender age these students have already lived long enough to learn some basic lessons of the real world. There are appropriate exceptions to be made in virtually every situation.

No country, no company, no department, and no individual is perceptive enough to foresee every future business scenario with such clarity to create a hard and fast policy, for every conceivable circumstance. It's foolish to think we can. Policies are made by fallible women and men just like you and me. So if the creators of policies are fallible, it is safe to assume that on occasion, the policies they create may be fallible as well.

Whenever I am the customer and I hear the "P" word (policy) being used by a person designated to service my needs, I have been conditioned to think the worst.

So what do I care what your policy says? I want to know what you can do for me. Rules are made to be broken. We all know it. The fact that you're using the policy statement with me now must mean that I am not an important enough customer for you to make an exception in my case. Well, if that's the way it's going to be, I can always take my business to someone who will appreciate me more.

Some might argue such thoughts are illogical and irrational. Maybe so, but those are still my thoughts. And I am like you. My conscious thoughts ultimately lead me to some specific course of action.

Willie's Way

When I climbed into Willie Watson's cab, it didn't take me long to sense there was something different about this service provider and the service experience he was creating. Initially, I couldn't explain it, but I could feel it. Then came the breakthrough moment. When Willie said he was changing his policies to accommodate me, the customer, I knew I was engaged in a unique service experience. One created just for me. As a result, my thoughts and attitudes changed accordingly.

Wow, I must be special. This guy really wants my business. He's bending over backward to accommodate me and my schedule. He's genuinely interested in me and my needs. How can I give him more of my business?

How did Willie do it? He took the "P" word out of the equation by showing his willingness to bend his own rules. Remember the situation? Before dropping me off at my hotel after the ride from the airport, Willie offered to return to my hotel the next day to transport me back to the airport in time for my departing flight. I had hesitated because I wasn't able to commit to a specific time. On the spot, Willie reworked his own service policy.

Willie could have said, "Phil, I'm sorry, but it's against my policy to come to the hotel and sit and wait for passengers." All the while thinking, *"Sitting and waiting for you would take too much time and frankly, it is just too risky. I don't want to run the risk of losing a possible fare waiting for you. I've learned the best policy for my business is to require that all potential passengers call for me when they are already standing on the curb, desperate for a ride. Then I get to them as quickly as I can, if I can. I really can't make an exception for you, because if I did something special for you, then everybody would expect me to do something special for them. And we all know that's no way to run a business."*

But that's not what Willie said and I'm sure it's not what Willie thought. When I explained that I couldn't guarantee an exact time I would be able to meet him for the ride back to the airport, Willie's sense of imagination, creativity, and inclination toward rule bending kicked into high gear. Let me remind you again what he said.

Bend the Rules, Sometimes

"Stop right there, Phil. If that's all you're worried about, I can help ya out. I'll be at the hotel at noon. If ya don't come out 'til 12:30, no problem. If ya don't come out 'til 1:00, I'll still be waitin'. Heck, Phil, if ya don't come out 'til 3:00 o'clock, I'll STILL be sittin' in this cab waitin' on ya. Now ya need to know something—I don't do this for everybody . . ."

That's where Willie won me over. He spoke the words directly to me. "I don't do this for everybody." Frankly, I didn't care if he was doing it for one other person—or a hundred. I didn't care how he did it—as long as he did it. And I didn't care why he was doing it for me—I just cared that he was.

People can bend the rules in a thousand different ways and almost all of the ways end up making someone feel special. On the other hand, inflexibility and the unwillingness to bend rules can result in customers feeling unappreciated, even manipulated.

Take a Minute to Think

"Thank you for calling [name withheld] Hotel. How may I direct your call?"

"This is Phillip Van Hooser. I have a reservation at your facility for this evening, but my flight has been delayed and now I won't be arriving until almost midnight. That won't be a problem will it?"

"Not at all, sir. We have your confirmed registration right here. If you would like, I can go ahead and schedule an airport pickup for you. Once you arrive, look for our white stretch limo just outside the baggage claim area. It will be waiting for you curbside."

Wow! Great! And a stretch limo to boot. Pretty impressive.

"Thank you so much. That would be great," I replied. Relieved, I gave the clerk my scheduled arrival time and hung up the phone.

Two flights and six and a half hours later, my plane touched down at my destination. Tired, I gathered my bags and headed outside as previously instructed. To my dismay, there was no limo in sight. In fact, the entire arriving passenger area was deserted. I headed back into the terminal and called the hotel again.

"Hello, this is Phillip Van Hooser. I was expecting a shuttle pickup at the airport. I scheduled it earlier this evening."

"Yes, sir. The driver is on his way to the airport now. However, there has been a little mix up . . ." the clerk replied, as his voice trailed off slightly.

"Mix up? What kind of mix up?" I asked suspiciously.

"Well, sir, we've had some computer problems and unfortunately, we have no room for you this evening."

"No room? I made this reservation more than six months ago," I countered. "Earlier tonight one of your clerks told me that my room was waiting. My confirmation number is 725341."

"I'm sorry, sir. There are no rooms available," the clerk repeated. "Our driver has been instructed to take you to the Comfort Inn across town for the evening. You'll be quite comfortable there and, of course, due to your inconvenience, we will take care of the room charges. Tomorrow evening we will have a room for you. I guarantee it," he said confidently.

Frustrated, I resigned myself to my fate for the evening and headed outside to wait for my ride. Soon, the complimentary white stretch limo was whisking me across town to the Comfort Inn. The ride was a quiet one, except for one bit of telling information shared accidentally by the limo driver. The driver, unaware of the reason given me earlier for my room cancellation, explained that a state political candidate and his entourage had arrived at the hotel for a political rally that evening and had decided to stay the night.

Computer problems, huh?

By the time I made it to my room, it was almost 1:00 a.m. Meetings were scheduled with my client for the next day. I tried to sleep fast.

Bend the Rules, Sometimes

Morning came quickly. I headed down to the hotel lobby for a quick bowl of Comfort Inn complimentary cereal. As I entered the lobby area, I heard the desk clerk asking those assembled, "Is a Mr. Van Hooser here?" I identified myself and was handed a note. The note said that the [name withheld] Hotel had called to let me know that my room would be available that evening. I was instructed to gather my belongings and come over for check-in. There was no indication a limo would be ferrying me this time.

As I read, I felt my irritation from the previous evening return. I turned to the Comfort Inn desk clerk and asked her to call the [name withheld] Hotel and inform them of my intentions to stay at the Comfort Inn for the second night and that I expected the [name withheld] Hotel to cover the bill. The clerk listened to my instructions, smiled, and gladly accepted the task. I stood by the counter as she made the call.

"Yes, this is Rebecca at the Comfort Inn," the clerk began. "One of the guests you sent over last night, Mr. Van Hooser, has asked that I call you and tell you he prefers to stay with us again this evening and he expects you to cover the room charges." She listened intently to the response from the other end before speaking again. "Ma'am, he's standing here right now. Why don't you tell him that?" she asked, before handing me the telephone receiver.

"Yes, this is Phillip Van Hooser. I was one of the confirmed guests whose reservation was voided last night. However, as your representative promised, the Comfort Inn proved to be quite comfortable and hassle free, and I have decided to stay here again this evening at your expense," I stated calmly.

"Sir, we can't do that," was the pleasant, but somewhat nervous reply. "Last night we had no room for you, but we do now, so we can't pay for your room tonight."

"Let me understand this. Last night it proved inconvenient for you to have me stay at your facility, and because that in turn inconvenienced me, you were willing to pay for my room here. However, now it seems it's no longer inconvenient for you, even though it's still inconvenient for me to repack my belongings and move again, but you've decided you won't pay for my room tonight. Is that about it?"

"Sir, I guess that's one way of looking at it. But, that's our policy. I'm sorry, but we still won't pay for your room tonight."

"Ma'am, would you like to take a minute to think about this situation again before you make your final decision?"

"That's not necessary, sir. The decision has been made," she said with a tone of finality.

"Fine," I said pleasantly. "Then I suggest as soon as you hang up this phone, you go tell your manager about this conversation and the decision you just made. If she wants to reach me, I will be resting comfortably here at the Comfort Inn." I handed the telephone receiver back to a beaming Comfort Inn desk clerk before heading for my bowl of cereal.

Less than five minutes later, I heard the desk clerk calling my name. "Mr. Van Hooser, there's a call for you." As expected, they had called in the heavier artillery. The Comfort Inn desk clerk tried to discreetly position herself nearby as I took the call. She was all ears.

"Mr. Van Hooser, we're very sorry about last night's mix up. But, we're sure you will be pleased with tonight's accommodations," the [name withheld] Hotel shift manager began sweetly.

"I know I will, because I'm staying here," I replied.

"I'm sorry, sir, but it's against our policy to pay for a second night when we have a room available," she stated more forcefully. "There are simply no exceptions. Is there anything else we can do for you?"

"Not if you don't intend to pay for my room. I have decided that I am staying here tonight," I said. "But, don't you want to take just one more minute to think about this situation?"

Bend the Rules, Sometimes

"No, we simply won't be able to satisfy your request," she said with the authority of her position.

"Well, then, it's only fair you know this evening I will be speaking at your facility to more than 200 local insurance professionals on the topic of customer service. I always build my presentations around practical examples. Tonight, I fully intend to talk about this situation. Goodbye." I hung up the phone and returned to my now soggy Fruit Loops.

Less than 10 minutes later, I received a second call from the shift manager. She called to tell me she had reconsidered my request and had decided to make an exception to their policy. They were now "more than happy" to cover the cost of the second night.

Too late. Once again, an unwavering focus on policy had destroyed another profitable customer relationship. The policies the [name withheld] Hotel claimed and trumpeted ended up being no more than smoke screens hiding their true service inclination. In the end, they opted to utilize a measure of imagination and flexibility, but only under pressure and only after the damage had already been done. By that time it was too late.

That's not "Willie's Way." Thankfully, some service professionals seem to know that instinctively. The following story goes a long way toward illustrating my point.

"He Will If He Really Wants to Sell Me Something"

Restrictive, often self-imposed policies have a tendency to create a sort of mental fog too many service providers have difficulty seeing through. Since the fog (policy) restricts their long-range vision (purpose) and they can't quite make out what awaits them on the other side (obstacle or opportunity), upon encountering the fog they simply stop and choose to travel no further (no flexibility). It's just not safe to continue on, they contend, until what's on the other side is known.

But fog is a mist, not a wall. It can certainly obstruct vision. And when fog is encountered, one should voluntarily slow his or her progress. However, it is important to continue to move forward, albeit cautiously. To stop dead in one's tracks in a fog-shrouded environment makes that person vulnerable to all that is approaching from both the front and rear. Again I remind you, fog is a mist. It can be penetrated. We must work to move through it. Invariably, as we move though it, we begin to realize the fog is lifting and we are able to see more clearly again.

Though Van Knight and Willie Watson certainly had never met, they both understood the importance of going the extra mile to satisfy the needs of their customers. They were able to maneuver through the fog of their own business policies. These were two gentlemen who were able to see clearly the professional value and personal benefit that bending the rules occasionally could offer them and their business activities.

My father was never destined to grace the pages of *GQ Magazine*. He liked to look nice, but he was never burdened by the constraints imposed by current fashion trends. Few men of his generation in our hometown of Princeton, Kentucky, were. My dad bought what he wanted or needed, when he thought he wanted or needed it. But throughout his life he continued to hate the activity of shopping—especially for clothes. Therefore, when he (and he alone) determined the time had come to buy new clothes, he would go all out, usually buying two or three suits at the same time with all the necessary accessories. Because his suits were all purchased together and not staggered, the suits (and ties and shirts) all went out of style at the same time. Such minor details were of little consequence to Joe Van Hooser. My dad shopped for clothes when the mood hit him.

One morning, the mood struck. Out of the blue, my father announced to my mother the time had come for him to buy some new "dress clothes." Mom agreed.

Bend the Rules, Sometimes

"Well, then," my father continued, "I want you to call Van Knight and tell him I'm coming down to buy a couple of suits." Van was the owner of The Villager, a local clothing store.

"Joe, you don't have to call Van. We can just get in the car and go down there. The store will be open 'til five."

"That's just it. I'm not going down there while they're still open. I want to go after they close. I don't like all those other people (a.k.a. shoppers and employees) looking at me while I'm trying on clothes. Just call Van and tell him I want to come in when he's the only one there."

My mother was amazed. "Joe, he's not going to keep the store open just for you."

Daddy's response was to the point. "He will if he really wants to sell me something."

Exasperated, my mother did as my father requested. She called Van and explained Daddy's rather unusual request. But, Van didn't seem to be taken back by it.

"Sure Barbara, have Joe come on down this afternoon just after five and we'll get him all taken care of."

That afternoon, Van Knight bent his store's rules. For one day he worked extended store hours for one solitary customer. I'm sure he didn't do it because he wanted to work late. He did it because that's what his customer asked and expected of him.

It must have been quite a sight to watch Van Knight serve the rather unique needs of my father as he moved from one rack of suits to another, slipping into and out of pants and jackets in an otherwise deserted store. Oh yeah, my dad did this dressed only in his underwear, choosing to forego the availability—and perceived confinement—of the private changing rooms.

Strange? Absolutely! But, did it result in additional business for Van Knight and The Villager department store? Sure it did. Did Van's customer leave this otherwise dreaded shopping experience in a positive frame of mind? It couldn't have been any better. Is it reasonable to expect the customer to return at some point in the future? Most certainly. Do you think others will hear about the positive experience? In fact, the experience soon transitioned into a family story we have told and retold for years. Countless other people have relived the experience by way of the story. Unbeknownst to him at the time, Van was involved in creating a "Willie's Way" moment.

Now you may be thinking that service flexibility such as this, if it still happens at all, only occurs in small towns where people do business with people they know well. That is simply not the case. Service flexibility such as this happens whenever and wherever true service professionals make it happen.

I Guess This Is My Lucky Day

I knew it was a little risky to wear jeans on this business trip. But it seems every time I wear nice clothes on a small airplane something bad happens. Rips, snags, wrinkles, coffee stains, grease, mud, ink—I've experienced them all. Maybe I was rationalizing, but it just seemed smarter (and certainly more comfortable) to wear more durable and less expensive clothes (i.e., jeans, a sweater, and tennis shoes) on this trip than to wear my business suit. Besides, there was no plan to see my client before the following morning's meeting anyway. I felt relatively safe.

I climbed off the little United Express puddle jumper at the Burlington, Iowa, airport. As I descended the plane's stairs onto the tarmac, I took a minute to stretch. The sun was in the last stages of departing for the day. The air was cool. It felt good not to be cramped up anymore.

I entered the small terminal. As I made my way to the baggage claim area I heard my name being called.

"Mr. Van Hooser? Phillip Van Hooser?"

Bend the Rules, Sometimes

I turned to see a stranger staring at me. He was immaculately dressed in a dark suit, starched white shirt, and a red power tie. His black lace-up shoes wore the business equivalent of a military shine. He was staring straight at me with a puzzled expression.

"Excuse me, are you Phillip Van Hooser?" he asked tentatively. The way he posed the question gave clear indication he was expecting something other than what he was seeing.

Oh my gosh. This must be my client. Why didn't they tell me they were planning to meet me at the airport? I thought all the program participants were going to assemble tomorrow. I don't look much like the picture of professionalism they expected when they hired me to address their meeting.

"Yes, I'm Phillip Van Hooser," I said, trying my best to overcome this less than stellar first impression.

"Mr. Van Hooser, my name is Paul. I've been asked to collect you and drive you to your hotel." Paul looked me up and down quickly and then asked, "You do have checked bags, don't you?"

I knew exactly what was on his mind.

"Yes, I was just headed for the baggage claim to get my suit bag," I responded. Paul looked somewhat relieved.

Together we made our way to the baggage claim area and exchanged small talk until the various bags from my flight began to appear. Within moments, the crowd had dispersed, the luggage was gone and my bags were still nowhere to be seen. Paul's fear returned with a vengeance.

"Mr. Van Hooser, your bags are not here. Do you realize that you are scheduled to speak to more than 200 local business leaders at breakfast tomorrow morning? This is the biggest economic development meeting of the year for us. It is fairly formal meeting. The governor spoke last year . . ."

With each new sentence he spoke, I could sense Paul working himself into a frenzy born of worry. But there was really no need for him to worry—

I was already worried enough for both of us! However, I was struggling desperately to appear calm.

"Paul, I'll walk over here and find out what's happening," I said, hoping he would get the hint and stay where he was until I returned. He didn't. As I turned and headed for the agent in charge, Paul was right beside me. His nervousness was making me more nervous by the moment.

"Yes, I just flew in from Chicago, but my bags don't seem to have made it," I said casually to the baggage agent, hoping to reassure Paul with my manufactured calm demeanor. I was almost certain it wasn't working.

"Yeah, we had some weight restrictions on your plane. If your bags didn't make it on this flight, they will come either on the last flight tonight or the first one tomorrow morning." Over my shoulder, I could hear Paul start to hyperventilate.

"Well, when does the next flight arrive tonight?" I asked.

"Ten-thirty. But honestly, I doubt they'll be on that flight. It's booked full. More likely they'll be here tomorrow morning."

"What time tomorrow morning?"

"Seven-fifty."

That's what I was afraid of.

"That won't help me. I speak at eight in the morning," I said, thinking out loud.

"Well, give me a description of your bags and where you're staying. But, don't count on them getting to you tonight. I'm almost positive it won't happen."

I wrote slowly trying to buy some time to think. I was upset, but this wasn't the time to show it. When I finished my assigned paperwork, I handed the completed form to the baggage representative and then turned to Paul.

Bend the Rules, Sometimes

"Paul," I said cheerfully, "I think I need to go shopping. Does Burlington have a mall with a men's store in it?"

Minutes later we were entering Turley's Menswear, in the West Burlington, Iowa, mall.

"Welcome to Turley's. How can I help you gentlemen tonight?"

The young man behind this question could have been no more than 22 years old. With his dark, slightly over-sized suit, he seemed a little overdressed for his position. But who was I to pass judgment? With my jeans, I was woefully underdressed for mine. But, I was counting on this young man to remedy that.

"What's you name?" I asked.

"Matthew, sir."

"Well, Matthew, I've got a problem and I believe you're just the man to help me solve it. I will be speaking to a very important group of businesspeople tomorrow morning and I need some clothes. Do you think you can help me out?"

"What kind of clothes?" Matthew asked.

"All of them," I replied. "Everything. A suit, shirt, belt, tie, socks, shoes—the whole shooting match."

The young man's eyes widened as he began to grasp the significance of the situation he had just fallen into. When I finished describing my need, Matthew looked me straight in the eye and said, "Yes, sir, I can help you. I guess this is my lucky day."

For the next 30 minutes or so, Matthew hustled me around the store collecting the only size 40 Regular suit on the premises. He found a white shirt my size and then convinced me that I was just the right person to wear the only bright gold tie in the store. He moved from rack to rack and back again with purpose and professionalism.

Willie's Way

As Matthew took control, Paul began to relax. Now, as this scenario continued to unfold before him, Paul seemed to be enjoying the proceedings immensely. Once Matthew had secured a belt and socks (Turley's didn't carry shoes—those would come from elsewhere), I presented him with the biggest challenge of all.

"Matthew, you're doing great. But, there is still one major obstacle to overcome. How are we going to get these pants hemmed tonight? Look at them. They are at least 12 inches too long."

"Sir, don't you worry about that at all," he responded confidently. "I intend to hem these pants for you."

Matthew didn't look like any seamstress I had ever known. Sensing my obvious suspicion, he suddenly hoisted his leg in front of me and pointed to the cuff in his pants.

"Sir, I did that myself," he said proudly, "And I'm going to do just as good a job for you. It's slow in the store tonight. I have to be here until we close at nine. So, I will work on them until we close and then I will deliver them personally to you at your hotel. You go have dinner and relax. I'll take care of everything."

Matthew's confidence impressed me greatly. My total purchases at Turley's Menswear that evening came to $312.87. I gave Matthew my credit card and where I was staying before heading out in search of shoes and supper.

Later that evening, at exactly nine-thirty I answered the knock at my hotel door. There stood Matthew, just as he had promised, grinning and holding my new suit—the one with the perfectly hemmed pants. I thanked him and rewarded him for his willingness to work outside the conventional rules. I went to sleep that night thinking of Matthew's extra effort.

Just after midnight, I was awakened by another knock at my hotel room door.

Startled, I sat straight up in the bed. "Who is it?" I demanded to know.

Bend the Rules, Sometimes

"United Express. Your bags arrived."

Two different companies had exceeded my expectations in the same evening. They did so based on the extra efforts of two of their frontline service professionals. Both of these pros were just doing the basic job assigned them when the opportunity presented itself for them to prove their professionalism. However, to do so they had to step outside their prescribed way of doing things. They had to bend the rules of their organization to accommodate the unique needs of the customer. Matthew went above and beyond the call in hemming my pants and delivering my new suit to me on short notice. The United Express baggage claim agent also understood and appreciated the need I had for my clothes and he did what was necessary to see that I had them before my engagement the next morning.

Putting It Into Practice

Some have been trained and conditioned to believe bending rules and going against established policies, for any reason, is akin to organizational heresy. They would never allow themselves to be guilty of such an atrocity.

However, I contend that bending rules is different than breaking them. I am not advocating wholesale organizational lawlessness. I am encouraging you to look for the unique service opportunities around you. The ones that might require a little imagination and innovation. Willie did it by being willing to sit and wait. Van did it by staying late. Matthew did it by taking needle in hand. The baggage agent did it by delivering past my point of expectation. And I believe you can do it, too.

Here are three points to consider:

1. Evaluate which policies, rules, and procedures are pliable and which are not.

Take a minute or two right now to list on paper the specific policies, rules, and procedures within your organization that are *never* to be breached. To do so would simply be too risky, too costly, illegal, immoral, unethical, or just plain wrong. Issues involving safety matters, inventory counts, tax reporting, and personnel decisions fall into this category. Now list those activities in which we are involved, especially the ones that impact internal and external customers, which have more room for independent decision making. These are the policies, rules, and procedures that can be bent on occasion to satisfy the needs of your customers.

2. Take a minute to think.

Decisiveness is a wonderful attribute. However, shortly after the moment in which a service decision was made, people are no longer concerned with *how long* it took us to make a particular decision, but rather *why* we made it. Before committing to a course of action, take a minute to think about the specific long-term ramifications of the action. Ask yourself, "What is the best thing that can happen if I respond to a customer in a particular way?" Then follow that question with, "What is the worst thing that can happen if I respond to a customer in a different way?" A minute of thought may save hours, days, weeks, months, and even years of regret.

3. Pick your words carefully.

Be careful what you say. Your customers are actually listening. Remember, if you are prone to say, "policy says . . ." at the drop of a hat, what the customer is actually hearing is, "big company, little me; their Goliath versus my David." Therefore, even when it is necessary to communicate the policy line, never say "policy says . . ." again. In its place say, "This is what I can do for you . . ." Now what the customer hears you saying is, "I am your friend. I am your advocate." Pick your words carefully. You will have to live with the results they produce.

Secret # 6

Make the Last Few Seconds Count

What do ya think?
Ya want me to come get ya or not?
— Willie Watson

What happens last usually matters most. It always has. I believe it always will, especially in the service we offer others.

In political contests, great numbers of undecided voters wait to make up their minds regarding which candidate they will support until the "last days of the campaign." Class standings are determined and academic scholarships won or lost dependent on scores earned during "final examinations." Movies live on in the minds of viewers, often due to a character's "famous last words." Who can ever forget Rhett Butler's famous last words in *Gone with the Wind*? "Frankly, my dear . . ."

Why is that? Why isn't day one of our senior year in high school as emotion-filled as graduation day? Why don't baseball players run and celebrate joyously after the first pitch of Spring Training instead of waiting until the last out of the World Series?

Maybe it's because individuals don't have as much of themselves invested in the activity in the beginning as they do at the end. Maybe it's because the outcome of the event is often not determined until the last few seconds. Or maybe it's because of that unseen, unknown "something" that allows special individuals to reach deep within themselves as they focus their last bit of energy, emotion, and effort on the task at hand, allowing good things, amazing things, even heroic things to happen at the very end.

Whatever the reason, the end, the finish, the close, the conclusion, the last few seconds—very often, that's where the real action is to be found.

The same is true of customer relations. More often than not, what happens last is what the customer remembers longest. Did the customer get his or her needs satisfied, were their expectations met? In the end, they will remember the outcome longer than they will the process.

My entire experience with Willie Watson has proven to be quite memorable. But the primary image that remains indelibly etched in my mind is that of Willie, after showing considerable flexibility in his service options to me, asking me point blank, ". . . what do ya think? Ya want me to come get you or not?"

Willie was working to close the deal. In so doing, he gave me a choice. I could either accept the service he was offering or I could reject it. The choice was mine, but Willie made sure his last words made me know I had to choose.

True service professionals recognize that customers have a multitude of choices available to them. Frequently, customers will base their specific choices on what happens last in the service experience, not what happens first.

"You Don't Expect Us to Give Our Services Away Do You?"

The deadline for submitting the required paperwork for our graduating son's college applications was fast approaching and we were not ready. Each application required a copy of our current year's income tax return. Yet, we had been unable to complete and file our taxes due to a single missing piece of critical information. Specifically, during the tax year in question we sold a few shares of stock that had been purchased 15 years earlier. Of course, we knew how much the stock sold for, what we couldn't remember was how much we paid for the stock initially. Without that information, a capital gains

Make the Last Few Seconds Count

calculation could not be made and our taxes could not be filed. With the college deadlines looming, my wife was getting a bit frantic. The pressure was on to find that information.

"Phil, you've got to call the brokerage company you used to purchase the stock," Susan urged.

"Why don't you go ahead and call them?" I asked.

"I tried, but the stock was purchased in your name. Therefore, they tell me they can't talk to anyone but you."

"Okay, okay. I'll try to call them today."

And try I did—again and again. Each time I dialed, an automated answering machine would pick up and begin to spew out the vast array of options available to callers. The more carefully I listened, the more confused I became. Finally, I heard the words I was listening for. "For customer service assistance, please press three."

Finally! That's exactly what I need—a little customer service assistance.

But my adventure was not yet over. After pressing "three" as prompted, the phone rang a few more times before I heard yet another automated voice. "I'm sorry all of our customer service representatives are busy assisting customers at the present time. The anticipated wait time is 16 minutes. Please continue to hold."

Sixteen minutes? They've got to be kidding. I don't have 16 minutes to waste sitting here hoping to eventually hear a human voice. This is ridiculous. I'll call back when I have more time and it's not as busy.

I hung up.

A few minutes later, Susan came into the office and asked, "Have you talked with them?" I explained that I had tried and that I would try again later that morning. I did try again that morning and twice that afternoon, each time experiencing the same outcome. "I'm sorry all of our customer service representatives are busy..."

The next morning I intentionally arranged my schedule to arrive at the office early so that I could call at exactly 8:00 a.m. EST. (I live in the Central Time zone.) To my surprise, a human being in the customer service department actually answered the phone. I explained my dilemma. In turn, he explained that since my stock purchase took place more than five years before, my records had been moved to a long-term storage facility off site. But, if I faxed a RFI (request for information), they would then be happy to research it for me. But, there was a catch. He explained it could take up to 10 days for the information to be forwarded to me.

With Joe's college application deadlines fast approaching, I would have liked a quicker turn around, but I could still live with 10 days—barely. I faxed the information they needed within the hour. Then I sat back and waited.

Ten days passed and I had heard nothing. Exasperated, I began the telephoning process again while experiencing the same automated frustrations as before. Nevertheless, I kept trying. Eventually, I was connected with a human being.

"Yes, my name is Phillip Van Hooser. I spoke with someone in your department more than a week ago about a request for past stock purchase information..." I went on to explain the entire situation and the actions that had already been taken. When I finished the explanation, the woman informed me that she would have to put me on hold. She gave me no indication as to why the hold was necessary or how long it would last. For the next 10 minutes, I sat in telephone limbo waiting for her return. Her eventual return yielded bad news.

"Sir, we have no record that you ever filed a formal RFI," she began.

I immediately felt the perspiration forming on my forehead. I felt my face flush. I struggled to maintain my composure.

Make the Last Few Seconds Count

"How can that be?" I asked. "I followed the directions your colleague gave me. I have been waiting patiently for 10 days like he told me. My time is running short. I need that information and I need it now," I said emphatically.

"Sir, we don't keep those old records here. If you wish to have us conduct a historical search, you must say so in writing and send us a check for five dollars. The five dollars is our search fee. Once we receive your check, we must wait five working days to make sure the check clears. After that, it will take three to four weeks to conduct the search based on our current backlog of similar requests."

I couldn't believe what I was hearing! They expected me to wait five days for a five dollar check to clear. Then another three to four weeks for them to process my request, plus the 10 days I already have invested in this little project. *I'll bet by the time I actually get the information Joe will be about ready to graduate—from college!*

I tried to stay cool. I really did.

"Ma'am, time is of the essence for me," I tried to explain rationally. "I still have several thousand dollars sitting in an open account with your firm. Is there any way you could waive the five dollar fee or withdraw it from my account and get on with the search?"

I will never forget her next words. Just thinking about them now causes me to shake my head in disbelief.

"I'm sorry, sir," she said. "I can't make an exception for you. You don't expect us to give our services away do you?"

Give your services away? I have been paying your firm a maintenance fee for 15 years! This is the very first request for any type of service I have ever made. There is still money in my account. We're taking about FIVE DOLLARS! I can't believe my ears.

I suppose in some cobweb-filled corner of her mind, the logic of her last statement made perfect sense to her. But, for me it simply served as her last words. I'd had enough. It was time for me to move on with my life. And guess what? I did move on.

This customer service representative's last words sent me scurrying to her firm's competitor. I closed my account with her firm, reallocated my resources with the competitor and moved on.

Willie Watson wasn't a financial consultant. The individual cash transactions with his passengers didn't involve thousands of dollars. But he had enough common sense to know that you don't throw away thousands of dollars of business to get five. He knew if I agreed to ride with him back to the airport that he just doubled his sales revenue on this one passenger. If that scenario repeated itself often enough, his driving calendar would stay full and his bank account would grow accordingly.

I continue to be amazed at how masterfully some service professionals orchestrate the last few seconds of a professional encounter while other service providers ignore the significance of the last few seconds all together. The difference in approaches can make all the difference in a long-term business relationship or one that simply might have been.

They Try Harder . . . And It Pays

September 11, 2001, was a terrible day. The horrific images of the planes hitting the twin towers and the unfolding tragedy that followed in New York, Washington, and that isolated field in Western Pennsylvania are indelibly etched in the minds of millions.

I was in Chickasha, Oklahoma, wrapping up an assignment with a manufacturing client that Tuesday morning. Two days earlier, I had flown into Oklahoma City, rented a car, and driven southwest to the Chickasha facility. Later that day, I was scheduled to fly from Oklahoma City back to Orlando, and pick up my car, before driving south to Ft. Myers, Florida, for a speaking engagement on Thursday morning.

Make the Last Few Seconds Count

However, like thousands of others, my plans changed. As the full magnitude of the tragedy began to unfold, it was announced the Federal Aviation Administration had grounded all aircraft indefinitely. I wouldn't be flying back to Florida any time soon. I had to quickly figure out some other way to get to my Ft. Myers engagement in less than 48 hours.

My Avis rental car was due to be returned to the Oklahoma City airport on the afternoon of 9/11. I decided that wasn't going to happen. I needed that car. I admit I didn't take time to read the renter's agreement and consider all the ramifications of my snap decision. I just figured when the appropriate time came I would ask forgiveness, not permission.

Encountering another stranded business traveler, I agreed to take him to his home in Nashville, Tennessee, on the condition that he help with the driving responsibilities. He agreed and we were soon motoring together from Chickasha to Nashville (713 miles). About 11 hours later, we arrived at his home in the suburbs of Nashville. He graciously offered me the opportunity to rest before continuing. I slept for a few hours before setting off on the solo leg of the trip to my home in Ocala, Florida (610 miles). Ten hours later, I pulled into my driveway where I was greeted by my wife, kids, and one of my buddies. Like the Pony Express, he was there to offer driving relief. Minutes later, he and I were back in the car headed for Ft. Myers, Florida, (223 miles) and four more hours.

The plan went off without a hitch. Over 1,500 miles driven in less than 30 hours. Besides being dog tired, I made it to my destination in the prescribed time period. I fulfilled my professional obligation. And I gained a new appreciation for the love, support, and kindness of family, friends, and even strangers during difficult times.

It wasn't until we left Ft. Myers headed for the Orlando airport (200 miles) to pick up my personal car that I started considering all the possible ramifications of my extended trip.

Willie's Way

When I turn this car back in, what's going to happen? I hope I'm not arrested for grand theft auto. I wasn't authorized to drive the car out of the state of Oklahoma. They could give me grief about not dropping the car in Oklahoma City like I was supposed to do. But, come on, my options were limited. What else could I do? What really worries me is how much are they going to charge me for keeping the car five days and driving almost 2,000 miles? Five days . . . let's see . . . it could be as much as $500, $600 maybe even $700. If it is, I guess I'll just have to pay it. What other option do I have? I had to get home.

The Orlando International Airport was all but deserted. With all flights still grounded throughout the United States, this usually bustling convention and vacation hub now sat eerily quiet. The only activity to be found was at the various rental car receiving areas.

We slowly navigated our way through the maze of orange cones strategically placed throughout the near empty airport parking garage. Following the signs marked "Avis Returns," an attendant motioned us to the front of the line where we parked.

The moment of truth has arrived. Just be pleasant and let's see how this thing plays out.

"Any trouble with the vehicle, sir?" the attendant asked as we climbed out. It was the same question I had heard dozens of times before when returning rentals.

"No, It ran fine," I said, opting not to share any more information than was requested of me.

"Do you want to leave the charges on your credit card?"

"Sure."

The attendant then climbed into the vehicle and turned the key to check the ending mileage. This was the moment I had been dreading. Without another word, he climbed back out of the car and began punching buttons on his handheld computer. A few seconds later, the receipt began to appear from the handheld unit. The attendant ripped the receipt from the machine and read.

"Sir, that will be eleven hundred and . . ."

Honestly, I didn't hear the rest of the numbers he read. The eleven hundred were more than enough numbers for me.

Eleven hundred dollars! Relax, Phil. Breathe deeply. Just relax, I kept telling myself. Finally, I took a deep breath before beginning my explanation.

"Uhm," I began. "I was one of the folks that got stranded due to the tragedy. I drove the car all the way back from Oklahoma, but I wasn't expecting a bill like this. This is a problem," I said so calmly and evenly that I even surprised myself.

The attendant was every bit as calm and composed.

"Sir," he said with a big, toothy grin, "I don't solve problems around here, I just cause them. I think you'll want to talk to management." He pointed over my shoulder to the tiny manager's office located just behind me.

"Thanks," I said as I turned and headed for the hut. The manager saw me coming and met me half way.

"Yeah, I've got a bill here that's significantly larger than I expected," I began. "I was in Oklahoma and I didn't have any other way to get home. Do you think you can do anything to help me?"

"You're not the first one today," she said evenly. "Let me have your receipt and I'll see what I can do."

I handed her the receipt and she disappeared into the privacy of her tiny garage office. A few short minutes later, she reappeared with a refigured receipt in hand.

"See if that looks better to you," she said confidently.

I began to examine the revised receipt. The total charges had been reduced from $1,116.24 to $269.53. According to the receipt, I had driven 1,949 miles and had been charged $46.11 for fuel—I forgot to refill the tank before returning the car. I just laughed.

"Yeah, this is much better. Thanks a lot," I said, as I began to breathe easier.

"I'm glad we could help a good customer during difficult times," she said. "Thanks for traveling and for being loyal to Avis."

What great last words with which to end a business transaction, especially a transaction so potentially fraught with emotion. But what specifically did this "Willie's Way" service professional do that was so special? She told me she appreciated me as a customer. She acknowledged that it had been a tough few days for everyone. She seemed genuinely pleased to be able to offer help and emotional relief. Finally, she set the stage for an on-going business relationship. In fact, she thanked me for "being loyal to Avis."

Before that moment, I had never considered myself as "being loyal" to any car rental company. But her well-chosen final words planted a seed. She had made a difficult situation easier for me. Therefore, I wanted to continue to do business with Avis. In fact, I have. I have rented dozens of cars since September 2001. All except one have been through Avis. The single exception occurred in Salt Lake City. What happened? Avis was out of cars.

I just had a thought. You might by wondering how making the last few seconds count works during difficult, even hostile, service situations. Can a service professional maintain his or her composure and professionalism when the customer has already lost theirs? Certainly. And when done right, the outcome can be nothing short of astounding.

"Well, I'll Be Doggone"

Susan and I had just been seated in the crowded Peppermill Hotel restaurant in Reno, Nevada, when I noticed a group of five seated next to us. I quickly

Make the Last Few Seconds Count

guessed them to be a family—a father and a mother, accompanied by their three almost grown boys. For some reason, I caught myself imagining they were on a long overdue family vacation, possibly the last one they would share together before the boys left the nest, headed off to college or work.

As we settled in, I noticed the waitress delivering meals to the group. With great efficiency, four meals were distributed to the group of five. While the others were preparing to dig in, one of the boys sat looking a bit forlorn. The waitress jumped right on the problem.

"I'm sorry folks, I must've left the other meal in the kitchen. I'll run get it for you," she said, as she hustled away. Unfortunately, she returned a couple of minutes later empty-handed. I watched and listened as she broke the bad news.

"Umm, folks, I am so sorry but apparently the meal you ordered has been accidentally delivered to another diner. If you would like me to resubmit it, I will be happy to do so. But I wanted you to know that it will take about 10 or 11 minutes before it is ready."

An uncomfortable silence quickly fell over the table. No one seemed anxious to speak. The entire family looked to Dad. Finally, he spoke.

"Go ahead," he said in a rather gruff voice.

As the waitress turned to head for the kitchen, she and all the rest of us in the general area got an earful. The man started grumbling loudly, to no one in particular, about the poor service. In a matter of seconds, his complaints were punctuated by profanity.

I was mesmerized by the scene. Susan kept kicking me under the table, but I couldn't stop watching and listening. Though the grumbling eventually subsided, I wondered if the complaints would be rekindled once the boy's reordered meal was received. My antennae were up to see what happened next.

The boy's meal was eventually delivered, but not by the waitress. Instead, the restaurant manager set the plate in front of the young man. But more important than what he did was the professionalism he employed to do it. As soon as he had positioned the plate, he knelt beside the table next to the father. There was an obvious tension in the air.

"Folks," the manager began, "I want to personally apologize for the mistake we made with your order. That's not the way we normally do things around here, but we are human and mistakes do happen on occasion. Still, your meal was disrupted. You were upset and rightfully so. You came here to have a pleasant meal. We did not meet your expectations. I wish the situation had not happened, but since it did, the least I can do is let you know that all of your meals are on me tonight. Is there anything else I can get any of you?"

Everyone at their table looked shocked at the offer of five free meals. I quickly whispered to Susan, "See if you can find something wrong!"

Meanwhile, the father glanced around the table, then at the manager, before saying simply, "No, I don't reckon."

The manager then stood and said, "Well then, just know that my name is Tom and during your stay here at the Peppermill if you need anything—anything at all—not just here in the restaurant, you call and ask for me by name and I will do my best to make your stay more pleasant. Have a good evening." And he walked away.

What an interesting turn of events. I could hardly wait to hear the father's response to this new development. I watched as he sat quietly for a brief moment as if considering what had just taken place. Then, his head shaking slightly, he looked into the faces of his family before exclaiming, "Well, I'll be doggone!"

Those simple words said it all for me. They communicated both amazement and a sense of personal satisfaction. The manager had undoubtedly planned his last words carefully. In presenting them masterfully, he was able to turn a hostile customer into a satisfied, and possibly admiring, one. Right before all of our eyes, he was successful in snatching service victory from the jaws of service defeat.

Make the Last Few Seconds Count

Had the manager not planned and taken such positive final action, I can easily imagine the family returning to their home following their vacation, with the father complaining for weeks to all who would listen about the shabby service he received at the Peppermill. But by making those precious last few seconds count, the manager sent the family and particularly the father away in a much more positive state of mind. Can't you just see this guy at his favorite watering hole back home in Wolf Knuckles, Montana, holding court with his buddies and saying, "Yeah, we had a great vacation. You know, they've got some fine people at that Peppermill Hotel. If y'all ever get to Reno, you ought to make a point of staying there. And if you do, be sure to go in the restaurant and tell my buddy, Tom, I sent you!"

Making Friends by Serving Friends

I was frustrated. I was in the market for a gas-powered leaf blower. I had already tried the "big box" retailers in my area with no success. Unable to find what I was looking for and unable to find any employee willing, capable, or interested in assisting me, I decided to drive almost 20 miles from my home to a farm supply store in Fredonia, Kentucky (population 500).

As I pulled into the parking lot of Akridge Farm Supply, I immediately noticed parking spots were hard to come by. The business was a beehive of activity. Outside the store, people milled around a wide selection of push and riding mowers, as well as various displays of fencing, watering tanks, and building supplies. To me, it seemed every shopper had someone assisting him.

Inside, fully stocked shelves featuring a wide variety of products came into view. Fertilizers, pesticides, gardening implements, tools, veterinary supplies, work clothing, hardware, and much more were all available. All things one would expect from such a store. But there was also the unexpected. Adorning the walls were obvious bits of Fredonia's history. There were antique farm tools used by area farmers in bygone days. Framed pictures of local high school basketball teams, some more than four decades old. Even a child's wool baseball jersey, circa 1950, hung from the ceiling displaying the simple sewed-on block letters—FREDONIA. These simple touches gave the store environment a homey feel.

As I glanced around at the walls, a salesperson approached. She asked if she could help and I told her I was interested in the leaf blowers. She led me to a display as she continued to ask me questions. When I explained that our home had a large yard with more than 150 oak and hickory trees, she sprang into action. In no time, I was holding one of her top-of-the-line leaf blowers. The lady encouraged me to follow her outside, where she had me "start it up and see what you think."

For the next several minutes, I "test drove" that blower all over the parking lot. I was impressed, but not quite ready to make a buying decision. Then she offered me the option of taking it home and using it for the balance of the weekend, with no obligation to purchase. Though the blower's price was more than I had intended to spend, her flexible approach sold me. Soon I was at the cash register, credit card in hand, with my new blower and a few other "essentials." All totaled, I spent more than $300 that Saturday morning and left with a feeling that is all too uncommon these days. I felt satisfied. I felt like I had actually been served. I felt like this organization somehow appreciated my business. I went home and immediately put my new purchase to work.

The following Wednesday, correspondence arrived in the mail, hand addressed to me. The return address read, "Akridge Farm Supply." I was curious. I opened the envelope to find a formal "Thank You" note, dated May 27th (the Monday following my Saturday purchase) which simply read:

Dear Phil,

Thanks for buying the Echo Power Blower and other items from us on Saturday. We appreciate your business and friendship.

Sincerely,
Dean Akridge

Make the Last Few Seconds Count

I realized I was holding a note of appreciation from the owner of Akridge Farm Supply himself. I was amazed and thrilled. Here was a business, founded in 1933, who still understands the importance of making the last few seconds of any business transaction count. Though I didn't see Mr. Akridge during my visit to the store that day, the system was in place for him to know I had been there and had purchased something. As a result, he took a few seconds to let me know he appreciated my business. Will I shop there again? What do you think?

Many people wonder how the "little guys" can hope to compete with such fierce national competition as exists today. The answer is the same as it has been for over 70 years at Akridge Farm supply—creative, exceptional, extraordinary, uncommon, unexpected service!

Customers have always appreciated the way service professionals like Dean Akridge, the Peppermill restaurant manager, the Avis representative, and of course Willie Watson leave them feeling—and they always will!

Putting It Into Practice

Making the last few seconds count is a great way to leave a positive, lasting impression in the minds of customers. But how is it best done? The first step is to have an appreciative attitude and then be creative in how you express that attitude to others.

Here are three thoughts to help you focus on getting the most from those last few seconds:

1. Tell them specifically what you appreciate.

Most business interactions are casual and shallow. We have all learned to say, "thank you for your business." "Willie's Way" disciples need to go further. Dean Akridge thanked me, his external customer, specifically for "buying the Echo Power Blower." Be specific. Tell your project teammate, your internal customer, "Thanks for your help in pulling together the numbers for the regional manager's sales commissions," instead of, "Thanks for your help." Specificity proves you know and care about what others do for you.

2. Ask what else you can do to help them.

Never part company without asking what else your customer needs help with. Offering your assistance is the single best way to identify continuing or additional needs your customer (internal or external) may have. It also allows you the first shot at being the resource they may need.

3. Write them a note.

Whenever possible, write a note or send an e-mail to the customer (internal or external) in acknowledgment of the opportunity you had to offer them service. This follow up communication will likely be unexpected and therefore, much appreciated. It will cause the customer to think about you and your company (department) just a little longer and (hopefully) more positively than your competition.

Conclusion

The Magic of Service Professionalism

Phil, ya been talkin' about me, ain't ya?
– Willie Watson

Walk up to virtually any adult where you work, play, or shop and ask them to provide a definition for the concept of *service*. Most will be able to respond immediately with very little apparent thought or preparation. Expect to hear individual definitions that are simple and direct. They will all reference the customer, though some may use alternative terms such as client, member, citizen, constituent, or employee. No matter which terms are used, don't be surprised to hear definitions similar to the following:

Service is meeting and/or exceeding customer expectations.

This definition's essence is clear and unmistakable. Service is all about the customer. As a result, service providers who are truly interested in customers will always find ways to meet and exceed the customer's expectations. Those who are not truly interested in customers—the ones more interested in their own products, processes, or policies—will find or create multiple excuses to defend their obvious lack of customer focus. In the end, however, it really doesn't matter what excuses are offered to defend poor service practices. The excuses eventually prove to be the equivalent of smoke and mirrors—nothing more than an illusion—that customers will see right through.

So what is the primary difference between those who commit themselves to excellence in their customer service and performance versus those who seem to continuously muddle through their obligatory service activities? In a word, the difference is *professionalism*.

Willie's Way

Professionalism is my favorite word in the business vocabulary. Being thought of as a professional by those we serve is the single highest compliment any of us can receive regarding our work. Official titles and lofty positions are nice, rewarding, and ego-gratifying. But we position ourselves to truly make a significant service contribution only when we have differentiated ourselves from the masses of people wishing, praying, and claiming to be professionals.

Let's face it. Many individuals labor for decades in their jobs, never being mistaken for a professional. Others seem to have professionalism stamped all over them from the time they first assume their job responsibilities. So what makes an individual a professional? Consider the following definition:

Professionalism is the advanced level at which isolated individuals perform specific tasks and activities.

Take a moment to think about the various component parts of this definition. Better still, consider Willie Watson as a walking, talking, driving example of professionalism personified.

Professionalism is the "advanced level . . ."

Willie took the common services and attitudes expected of the average cab driver and bumped them up to an "advanced level." He was not content to be average or to do his job exactly as his counterparts had opted to do theirs. He recognized that he could do more for his customers and for himself. With equal parts service imagination and service effort, Willie easily distinguished himself from the dozens and dozens of other cab drivers I had encountered over the years who were content to be mediocre. His advanced level of service and performance caused him to stand out. He was memorable. He exceeded my expectations by going above and beyond.

Professionalism is the advanced level at which "isolated individuals . . ."

Willie understood "isolation." He worked in isolation hours on end, day in and day out. That's not to say he was out of touch or could not be reached.

The Magic of Service Professionalism

His dispatcher knew where he was and what he was doing at virtually any moment. But Willie was isolated from his supervisor. Therefore, he had either the option of "slacking off" when out of view of the peering eyes of management, or the option to "buckle down" and work to a different standard—his own—when the supervisor was no where to be found. Service professionals are independent decision makers, self-disciplined and committed to personal excellence, even when others are not watching.

Professionalism is the advanced level at which isolated individuals "perform . . ."

Willie Watson was not an actor. Far from it. I found Willie to be one of the most honest, unpretentious service professionals I've ever encountered. But the concept of "performance" is not reserved for thespians. Willie was on stage whenever a customer approached or occupied the seat of his cab.

Every job, task, or activity has a performance aspect to it. Whether we are the president of the United States, president of XYZ Corporation, president of the local Chamber of Commerce or just president of You, Inc., we all have jobs, tasks, and activities to complete. Some people are more understated in how they go about performing their jobs, choosing a meticulous, methodical or systematic approach. Others prefer to perform with more flair utilizing their unique sense of style, flamboyance, and timing. But in the end, professionals need to always remember someone is constantly watching them and their performance. The observer may be the customer, a supervisor, or an anonymous bystander. But a true pro recognizes he is always in the spotlight.

Professionalism is the advanced level at which isolated individuals perform "specific tasks and activities."

Some jobs are made up of singular, repetitive tasks and activities. Switchboard operators answer the phone. Order entry clerks process orders. Auto mechanics change the customer's oil.

Other jobs require a series of tasks and activities. For example, a salesperson may be expected to familiarize herself with the product/service, get to know the territory, initiate prospecting calls, follow up with interested respondents, develop customized proposals, provide product demonstrations, negotiate sales terms, process orders, track the production and delivery of the ordered products and/or services, and follow up with extraordinary service after the sale.

But whether the task and activity is simple or complex, our professionalism is ultimately determined by how well we do the little things at each level.

Willie Watson seemed to know that if he took care of the little things with his passengers, the big things would take care of themselves. Willie was unconcerned about whether I sat in the front or back seat. He saw to it that silence was replaced with conversation once the ride began. He asked pertinent questions and then listened intently to my answers in order to learn as much as he could about who I was and what brought me to town. Most casual observers would conclude these activities were little things. Yet, in the end, because Willie managed the little things so masterfully, I felt comfortable entrusting to him my bigger things—additional business.

And so it goes. Continuously meet and exceed the expectations of customers while constantly performing in an unmistakably professional manner and good things almost magically happen.

When Magic Isn't Magic after All

I was *supposed* to be helping my wife, Susan, with the Christmas shopping. Unquestionably, the pressures of the holiday season were bearing down on her. She had explained to me, more than once, there was still much to do and limited time available to get ready for the holiday celebration. To add to the stress of the season, Susan was, shall we say, "great with child." Already Mom to an exuberant month-old son, Susan, now five months pregnant, found herself standing in the midst of a bustling department store on a Saturday afternoon attending to holiday chores—on swollen ankles. It's safe to say Susan was not having a lot of fun.

The Magic of Service Professionalism

And I'll be honest. I wasn't making it easier for her. As she stood, sculpting her plan of attack with a "family and friend" gift list in hand, I, her beloved husband, stood nearby much too obviously disinterested in the whole process. Okay, I'll go ahead and admit it. Shopping is simply not one of the great passions of my life.

Why am I here? I kept wondering inwardly.

For once, I was wise enough to think *before* I spoke. I was certain, if pressed, Susan could have quickly and pointedly explained the separation of our marital and parental duties to me in no uncertain terms. Therefore, I kept the question to myself and instead, turned my attention to finding a way out of my current circumstance.

Surely, this place has a television display around here somewhere. Maybe the football game's on. If I could just slip away for a few minutes . . . The plan took shape quickly in my mind.

"Susan, what can I do to help you?" I asked directly.

My apparent sudden change of heart seemed to catch her off guard. She looked up at me, an obvious expression of hope and relief registering on her face.

"Phil, thanks for offering. I'd appreciate it if you'd see if you can go find appropriate gifts for your brothers. It would also help if you would take Joe with you."

Though my underlying intentions were slightly self-serving, I had to admit her requests were reasonable. I could surely find gifts that would satisfy my brothers, while at the same time entertaining an easily bored toddler.

"Done," I said.

"Good. I'll meet you over in the housewares section in 30 minutes," she countered. "Remember, we have a lot to do and not much time to do it."

I nodded and dutifully checked my watch just before heading off on my assigned quest with Joe.

For the next few minutes, Joe and I wandered the sporting goods department in search of gifts. With no immediate luck, we started our trek toward electronics (and the televisions) when Joe became distracted.

"Daddy, what's that?" he asked, pointing up the aisle ahead of us.

I looked and saw a sizeable crowd of adults and children huddled together, but I couldn't tell for what reason. Curiosity got the better of me.

"I don't know, Joe. Let's go check it out."

As we approached the group, it became easy to see what was attracting all the attention. An amateur magician had apparently been hired to entertain the small, but appreciative crowd with simple, sleight-of-hand illusions. As the show continued, we inched our way toward the front of the crowd where Joe could get a better view. He was mesmerized. He loved watching the young performer produce first cards, then coins, and finally, scarves apparently from thin air.

I was enjoying Joe enjoy the performance so much that I quickly lost track of time. The next thing I knew, I felt someone grip my arm firmly. I turned to face Susan. She could see I was empty-handed. I could see she was red-faced and frustrated.

"Phil, we don't have much time and you haven't bought a thing," she reminded me pointedly in a loud whisper. "What are y'all doing over here anyway?"

"We're watching this guy do magic," I lamely explained.

Susan's eyes flashed. She turned her attention briefly to the magician, before glaring back at me. Then with a clear note of disdain in her voice she opined, "Phil, you're not watching magic. You're watching some guy perform simple tricks he's been practicing for years. Now that he's good at them, you just want to believe it's magic."

The Magic of Service Professionalism

Susan was right. Magicians are simply masters of tricks and illusions. Though I didn't recognize it immediately, I have since come to realize that Susan's read on magic has similar applications that apply to service as well. Consider the various definitions of magic I have discovered.

Magic Defined

I consulted the *American Heritage Dictionary of the English Language (Fourth Edition)* concerning the definition for the word *magic*. The dictionary offered four distinct definitions.

> **Definition 1: Magic** . . . *The art that purports to control or forecast natural events, effects or forces by invoking the supernatural (charms, spells, rituals).*

To the best of my knowledge there are no charms, spells or rituals available on the market today to allow businesses or service providers to supernaturally control the activities and attitudes of their current or perspective customers. Since the master service professionals I know haven't earned their service reputations by reading tea leaves or shaking chicken bones, from a service perspective I tend to dismiss the value of this definition outright.

> **Definition 2: Magic** . . . *The exercise of sleight of hand or conjuring for entertainment.*

Admittedly, sleight of hand card tricks and pulling an occasional rabbit out of a hat can be entertaining diversions, even for customers. But will entertainment alone meet and exceed the expectations of discerning customers today? I don't think so.

> **Definition 3: Magic** . . . *A mysterious quality of enchantment (charm, attraction, delight, fascination).*

Let's face it, customers love to be charmed and delighted by professionals who have committed themselves to serving others. Still, customers expect more than a feeling—they expect more than an emotional connection with those entrusted to servicing their individual wants and needs. They expect something that is more tangible. They expect something they can see as well as feel.

Definition 4: Magic . . . *Possessing distinctive qualities that produce unaccountable or baffling effects.*

Here it is! This is the definition of magic that works best for me. It's more believable and universally applicable than the others. It's not based in the "woo-ooo-ooo" realm of the paranormal. It does not depend solely on entertainment or enchantment to yield its positive effects. This definition comes closest to explaining the mysterious, mystifying, almost magnetic effect Willie Watson and other "Willie's Way" service magicians have on their customers.

But wait a minute. "Unaccountable or baffling effects" can be expected when one practices diligently the six secrets outlined in these chapters. Therefore, that means the art of service professionalism isn't magic—it's a simple process masterfully applied. But then, as Susan reminded me, magic isn't really magic either.

Nevertheless, service professionalism can most certainly yield magical results.

Mythical Customer Service

One of the special benefits of my professional speaking and training career has been the opportunity to work with and learn from some of the best and most highly regarded service organizations in the world. One such organization is Augusta National Golf Club in Augusta, Georgia.

Even folks who don't play golf regularly recognize the significance of Augusta National as home to *The Masters*, one of the PGA's four major annual tour tournaments. *The Masters*, arguably the most sought after ticket in sports, is considered by many the premier golf tournament in the world, played annually on the premier golf course in the world. Players, analysts, and

The Magic of Service Professionalism

fans alike regularly describe *The Masters*/Augusta National experience in the most reverent of terms.

In April 2002, I had the wonderful opportunity to work behind the scenes at "the tournament" for 10 days to learn how my concepts of practical leadership and service professionalism could be applied and enhanced in a premier service setting.

During a pre-tournament conversation with Jim James, director of Club Operations for Augusta National, I was amazed by the myriad of details he shared that had to be attended to before, during, and after the tournament to guarantee its success. Attention to such details was intended to assure an idyllic experience for club members and their guests, players and their families, tournament sponsors and VIPs, the international media, tens of thousands of patrons, and a world-wide television viewing audience. I quickly learned nothing was taken for granted and no detail was so small as to be deemed insignificant.

Simple examples of Augusta National's commitment to service include their no commercialization policy. No printed or electronic advertisements, signs, banners, or billboards can be found on the grounds at Augusta National. It is feared such blatant promotion would ruin the serene, pastoral visual effect the Augusta National members and staff has so painstakingly worked to create.

Food concessions for the tournament (including drinks and the traditional pimento cheese and egg salad sandwiches) are sensibly priced. In fact, they are unbelievably reasonable as compared to the near price-gouging practices of too many other premier sporting and entertainment venues today. As a result, instead of patrons leaving the grounds at the tournament grumbling about how much they (over) spent for lunch, they are more apt to wander away disappointed the experience is over so soon.

Another interesting detail involves the *green* wrappers and containers specially made for the food concessions. Green is the prominent color in *The*

Masters logo. But green is also the color of grass. Therefore, when some careless patron drops his sandwich wrapper on the ground instead of in the available trash receptacles, the contrast of green wrapper against green grass is less obvious than if the wrapper were white, yellow, or some other distinctive color. When television cameras pan the immaculate fairways, greens and viewing areas during the tournament, the view truly is picture perfect.

I learned these and other interesting details during my one-on-one tournament orientation with Jim James. But Jim also introduced me to the concept of "mythical service," an elevated service distinction to which all service professionals and organizations should aspire.

"Jim, besides the obvious, are there other service benefits derived from Augusta National's unwavering attention to detail?" I asked innocently.

Jim thought about my question for a moment and then chuckled.

"Well, Phil, here at Augusta National we have learned that when you are unashamedly attentive to even the smallest details and the positive results are on display for the world to see, eventually people start giving you credit for being even better, more diligent than you are. I call that phenomenon 'mythical service.'|hr|"

"Mythical service? I'm not sure I understand what you mean," I replied.

"I'll give you two quick examples. As you have seen, we take great pride in maintaining and enhancing the natural beauty of the grounds here at Augusta National. Our groundskeepers have seen to it that if you walked the course today, you would be hard-pressed to find a single weed anywhere. Encircling the course there are thousands of azalea bushes. There is a common myth that each year, before the tournament begins, Augusta National groundskeepers ice down the azalea bushes at night to assure they will be in full bloom during the tournament. Of course, we could never orchestrate such an undertaking. Even if we could, we still can't fool Mother Nature. Those bushes bloom when Mother Nature tells them to bloom. Yet, people choose to believe we do."

The Magic of Service Professionalism

"Another example of mythical service here happened just a few days ago. I received a call earlier this week from an Augusta resident. This person saw helicopters hovering over the course for most of two full days. The choppers were there to tape aerial shots of the course's fairways and greens to be shown during the tournament's weekend television coverage. But I was actually asked if the helicopters were there to blow pollen off the tree leaves to accommodate those patrons who might suffer from allergies."

"Phil, because of our reputation for attention to even the smallest detail, people end up giving us service credit for things we could never control. They choose to believe what they want to believe. Of course, we're glad they believe special things about us. It's a nice problem to have."

A nice problem indeed. What was our favored definition of magic again? *Possessing distinctive qualities that produce unaccountable or baffling effects.* "Mythical service" is nothing short of magical by definition.

It Can't Get "Mulch" Worse than That

Willie Watson and other "Willie's Way" service professionals teach us that when we take care of the little things in service relationships, the big things tend to take care of themselves. But what happens when we don't take care of the little things? Well, too often they tend to become the big things that stand in the way of an on-going business relationship.

Recently, I began one of the jobs I dread each year. Our home sets on four acres of property. Bordering our home and scattered around the yard are several large flower beds. Each spring, it is my responsibility to see that mulch is spread on each of those flower beds. It's a big job. In fact, it takes more than thirty loads of mulch to adequately do the job. And it's an expensive job. Each load of mulch costs $25.

Recently, I discovered to my dismay that my regular source for mulch (located about 12 miles from my home) was indefinitely out of product. In searching for alternative suppliers, I discovered one about six miles from my house and a second one about 30 miles from my house. Due to the proximity and convenience of the one six miles away, I went there first.

"How much for your mulch?" I asked the attendant on duty.

"Thirty dollars a scoop," he replied.

"Thirty dollars?"

I wasn't expecting it to be that much. That's more than I'm used to paying. If I buy all 30 loads here, that will cost me at least $900. Is it worth it?

The attendant apparently read my mind.

"I know you can get mulch cheaper elsewhere," he said. "But this is high-quality mulch. We use a large bucket on a front-end loader to load the mulch on your trailer. A $30 scoop is one full bucket. The bucket will be full and rounded up with mulch. You can be sure you will get your money's worth."

I stood and thought for a moment before responding.

That's still considerably more than I expected to spend. But, I'd probably spend more than $5 a trip in gas driving all the way out to the other place and back. I'm here. The mulch looks good. This is convenient. I might as well just get the mulch here.

"Okay, go ahead and load me up. By the way, you will be seeing a lot of me for the next few weeks. I will need almost 30 loads to finish this job."

Right there I made and communicated a $900 buying decision.

"Well, we're glad to help you out," he replied cheerfully.

The attendant called for a front-end loader driver who came out and loaded two full scoops on my trailer. I went in, paid the manager on duty the $60 fee, and was on my way.

The Magic of Service Professionalism

Less than an hour later, I had unloaded the mulch and was back for another two scoops. I parked my trailer near the mulch pile but was unable to locate either the initial attendant or the gentleman who had loaded me earlier. I went inside the store and found the manager on duty—the same one I had paid on my first trip.

"I need another couple scoops of mulch. But, I couldn't find anyone to help me outside."

"Yeah, they're both gone for the day. I'll have to load it for you," he said with little obvious enthusiasm. "You can go ahead and pay now if you want to."

I agreed and forked over another $60 payment. Although this was my second encounter with this individual in less than 60 minutes, there was no small talk, no questions about what I was doing with the mulch and no apparent sense of appreciation for the new-found business he was experiencing. The manager simply processed the transaction in silence.

I walked outside and waited. The manager eventually appeared and climbed behind the wheel of the front-end loader. I could immediately tell he wasn't terribly comfortable operating this piece of equipment. After two or three false starts and quite a bit of back and forth maneuvering, I watched as he finally approached the trailer with a bucket approximately two-thirds full of mulch. He dumped his load in my trailer and returned to the mulch pile for another scoop. By now, he was getting the hang of it. He returned to my trailer with the second scoop—this one full and rounded up. As he dumped the second scoop of mulch, he waved casually as he backed away. His mannerism indicated he believed the transaction to be finished. But as far as I was concerned, it wasn't. I approached the loader.

"Your first bucket was not quite full," I shouted over the din of the front-end loader's engine. "Would you mind giving me just a little more?"

It wasn't what he said first that bothered me. It was what I saw first. Whether his nonverbal communication was intentional or unintentional, I will never know. But one thing I know for certain. I saw it with my own eyes.

I watched this manager look at me, roll his eyes, shake his head slightly, and then turn away from me for a split second. In my mind, there was no mistaking this nonverbal message.

He thinks I'm trying to cheat him. He thinks I'm trying to get more than I deserve—more than I paid for.

I was upset immediately.

He shut the engine off. Then with a discernable measure of disgust in his voice, he said, "No, you got a full load."

"No, I didn't," I said flatly. "I stood right here and saw that the first bucket was not full. It was considerably less than what the driver gave me on my first trip here earlier this morning."

"Then he gave you more than he was supposed to," he countered quickly, with a defensive tone noticeable in his voice.

I couldn't believe what I was hearing. This was not a high-priced problem. To fix this problem, to satisfy this customer, would have cost almost nothing. I would have been satisfied with any extra amount he might have chosen to give me. Instead, he blew the opportunity.

I just stood in silence for a moment looking at him. There were a number of things I could have done. I could have ranted and raved in an effort to prove my point. I could have demanded he unload my trailer and issue me a refund. I could have lodged a complaint with the owner. Instead, I did what I imagine the vast majority of customers would have done under similar circumstances. I just turned and headed for the truck.

As I walked away, I heard the engine of the front-end loader start. I heard him shout after me, "Alright, I'll give you more if you want it."

It was too little, too late. I just shook my head, got in my truck, and drove away.

The Magic of Service Professionalism

Guess what? Believe it or not, that shortsighted manager was a magician, too. With two little gestures and a few ill-conceived words, he magically made business—POOF—disappear. He made $120 off me and then stood and watched as another $800 vanished into thin air.

Every customer interaction has the potential to be memorable. With the application of a little thought, imagination, and flexibility, it might occasionally be elevated to a magical realm.

Experiencing a Magical Moment

"This will be our annual customer service appreciation luncheon. Mr. Van Hooser, we want this to be a special meeting. There will be 1,500 of our customer service representatives in attendance. We want your presentation to give them all something to think about and then something to remember. Do you think you can help us out?" the meeting planner asked.

I smiled as I replied, "I certainly do. This is going to be fun."

November 6, 2002, found me standing on stage in front of hundreds of BlueCross BlueShield of South Carolina customer service professionals. My objective was simple. I was there to remind them of the real-life practical aspects of professional customer service that could help make them—and their company—better at servicing customers.

As I had done with audiences all over the United States for more than five years, I shared the practical lessons of service professionalism illustrated by my favorite cab driver, Willie Watson. Like every audience before who had heard the "Willie story," this one was fascinated by the impact one person can have on another if that person's straightforward, uncluttered objective is unselfish service. They laughed while they learned from the example of a cab driver with whom none of them had ever ridden. The program proved to be a wonderful experience for all of us.

But in the end, it got even better.

Willie's Way

I concluded my remarks that day in Columbia, South Carolina, this way. "By his example, Willie Watson taught me much about the practical nature of servicing customers. Now, I hope, by my words, he has taught you something, too. I enjoyed having the opportunity to meet Willie Watson in person. Now I hope you will enjoy meeting him in person, too. Ladies and gentlemen, I present to you, a true service professional, Willie Watson."

An audible gasp was heard throughout the room. To that point, many may have thought my "Willie Watson character" was a product of my imagination—some sort object lesson created to better illustrate the points of my service presentation. Others in the room might have accepted Willie Watson as the real person he was, but with absolutely no idea or thought they might one day meet him.

The audience's collective gasp gave way to applause. The appreciative applause soon gave way to a thunderous ovation that went on and on. Fifteen hundred people were standing, some standing on their chairs in hopes of getting a look at Willie. Everyone in the room was on their feet—everyone except Willie. Willie continued to sit, somewhat overcome by the attention and adulation not normally doled out to a cab driver.

Finally, with encouragement from me, Willie rose from his seat at the table in front of the stage and accepted the appreciation of those in the room. After the program, dozens of people stood in a line six and seven deep to meet and greet Willie and to shake his hand.

Finding Willie had been a challenge. Though I had spoken *of* Willie to thousands of people, representing dozens of service-focused organizations in the previous five years, I had not spoken *to* Willie since our first chance meeting. After numerous calls to numerous cab companies and shuttle services in and around Columbia, South Carolina, I finally located the man himself. Even more amazing, Willie remembered me from our one and only meeting.

"Willie, this is Phillip Van Hooser. I don't expect you to remember me. I rode in your cab about five years ago. You picked me up at the airport and

The Magic of Service Professionalism

took me back the next day. I was in town to . . ." Willie interrupted me before I could explain further.

"If I'm rememberin' right, you were that speaker, weren't ya?"

I have never been more flattered to be remembered by anyone. And as illogical as it may seem, somehow I wasn't surprised by his flawless recall.

I explained to Willie what an impact he had made on me during our initial meeting. I explained that I had been using him as an example in my customer training sessions for the past five years. Willie was shocked. I invited him to join me for the BlueCross BlueShield program so he could hear the story firsthand. He accepted the invitation and brought along his wife and daughter. It was an unforgettable experience.

When the crowds had finally departed that day, I found myself alone with Willie in the cavernous hall. Where hundreds had stood and cheered just minutes before, it was now just the two of us.

"Willie, thank you for being such a good service example. The folks loved you," I offered. "I hope you enjoyed the experience, too."

Willie looked at me through misty eyes.

"Phil, oh yes. This was the best day of my life. It was just like magic."

Soon Willie was chauffeuring me back to the airport. Upon arrival, we parted company as friends. As I sat in the gate area awaiting the flight that would take me out of Columbia, my thoughts drifted back to that earlier trip into Columbia, five years prior and the chance meeting with Willie Watson.

The customer service lessons I have been sharing with audiences since that day were revealed through Willie's actions in minutes, not hours, days, months, or years. On stage that day, before an audience of hundreds, I had been given the opportunity to practice what Willie Watson and so many other service professionals had taught me over the years.

Acknowledge the customer immediately, redefine routine activities, give customers my undivided attention, listen, think, and use common sense, bend the rules occasionally and make the last few seconds count. Service professionalism is easy, effective, and magical when it's done "Willie's Way."

About The Author

Phillip Van Hooser, MBA, CSP, CPAE

Phillip Van Hooser is committed to helping organizations transform their business outcomes by transforming the talent of their people. Using his commonsense approach to leadership development and service professionalism, companies experience strengthened employee and customer relations, along with heightened levels of engagement and better bottom line business results.

Phil is an accomplished speaker, author and business leader. He has written multiple books including *We Need to Talk: Building Trust When Communicating Gets Critical* and *Leaders Ought To Know: 11 Ground Rules for Common Sense Leadership*. His leadership development work helps top U.S. companies and small-town entrepreneurs alike deliver on their commitments to employees, customers and shareholders.

Phil is a 30+ year member of the National Speakers Association and has been inducted into the CPAE Speaker Hall of Fame. In 2014, Phil started a non-profit initiative for the development of rural-area millennial leaders. Calling it one of the most rewarding efforts of his career, Phil serves as advisor, leadership instructor, mentor and coach for 25 to 35 year olds seeking leadership growth and training.

Also by Phillip Van Hooser

Leaders Ought to Know®:
11 Ground Rules for Common Sense Leadership

We Need to Talk:
Building Trust When Communicating Gets Critical

You're Joe's Boy, Ain't Ya?
Life's Lessons for Living, Loving & Leading

For More Details, Please Contact:

Van Hooser Associates, Inc.
PO Box 643
Princeton, Kentucky 42445
hello@vanhooser.com
+1-270-365-1536

Build Your Performance, Profits and People.

Ways Phillip Van Hooser Trains & Inspires the People Who Transform Your Business

Association / Corporate Keynote Presentations
Professional Development Training
Online Leadership Development Courses

For More Details, Please Contact:

Van Hooser Associates, Inc.
PO Box 643
Princeton, Kentucky 42445
hello@vanhooser.com
+1-270-365-1536

Other Ways to Connect:

www.vanhooser.com
www.linkedin.com/in/phillipvanhooser
www.youtube.com/philvanhooser
www.facebook.com/philvanhooser
www.twitter.com/philvanhooser